THE BRIDGE

Crossing Over to Your Greatest Joy in the Middle of Your Darkest Night

DEBORAH RUTH CIFRANIC

ISBN 978-1-64258-663-3 (paperback)
ISBN 978-1-64258-665-7 (digital)

Christian Faith Publishing, Inc.
832 Park Avenue
Meadville, PA 16335
www.christianfaithpublishing.com

Printed in the United States of America

This book is dedicated to Jesus, who makes everything possible. He is my inspiration and my motivation. Without Him, I would never have written this book.

CONTENTS

Acknowledgments

My husband Mark, thank you for encouraging me to write this book for more than a decade and for being my biggest cheerleader. I could never have done this without your consistent love, prayers, and support.

My daughter Allie Hampton, my sister Karen Ballard, and my friends, John and Dorene Amstutz, thank you so much for taking the time to read through my first draft and for helping me with the editing process. Your encouragement, suggestions, and constructive criticism gave me the confidence I needed to finish this book. I can't express to you how grateful I am for your time, insight, wisdom, love, and prayers.

My friend, Lynnette Titus, thank you for giving me the emotional support and the practical tips I needed to get this book started. I don't know if it would have happened without your love, prayers, and advice.

My God, I will be forever thankful for your unconditional love and grace. You have sustained and empowered me through every trial and tragedy, and blessed me with abundance, even though I'm so undeserving. Thank you for filling me with your Holy Spirit, who has enabled me to write this book. May it all be for Your glory.

INTRODUCTION

The Bridge

If you have ever felt depressed, suicidal, anxious, fearful, angry, heartbroken, grief-stricken, or anything else that stood in the way of feeling happy, my heart aches for you. I can understand your pain. I have been there. I long to see you free from those toxic feelings.

Grief and sadness are a regular part of our earthly existence. Life can be full of tragedies, and during tragic circumstances, those human emotions are completely understandable, and even expected. But tragic circumstances don't have to stand in the way of our joy. It may seem impossible to believe right now, but you truly can experience joy in all

9

circumstances. I have discovered that there is a way to remove the obstacles to joy and to be rid of them once and for all.

I know it's easy to be skeptical, especially if you have battled those feelings for many years as I had. Nothing seemed to really help me. I tried finding joy through relationships, work, service, possessions, money, travel, medication, therapy, self-help books, exercise, and even food. Some things made life more enjoyable, or at least tolerable. But nothing truly filled me with the lasting joy I was looking for, until I found "the bridge."

There is a bridge that can lead you out of your pain and into a new life, a life filled with joy. It's not a long bridge, and it's not extremely difficult to cross, but I have found that it can be very hard for some people to find. It has been hidden well, covered by the weeds and debris of the world we live in. It is engulfed in a heavy fog, making it almost impossible to recognize, particularly during the darkest nights.

Once the bridge has been found, many still won't attempt to cross it, feeling uncertain of the benefits. Blanketed in fog, the bridge appears useless and insignificant. Only the first plank is clearly visible, yet every plank must be crossed in order to get to the other side. At first, there is no tangible proof that the bridge leads to anything worthwhile. Crossing it requires belief, bravery, and perseverance. Many turn away.

But for those who are desperate enough to find a way out and take that first step, a miracle occurs. With each step of faith, a new plank is revealed, and the bridge is eventually crossed.

The blessings and benefits of crossing over the bridge are indescribable. There is a whole new life available to those who are courageous enough to make the journey. It is a life full of power, success, love, joy, peace, and so much more. It is an incredibly rewarding and fulfilling life, a life truly worth living.

Dear friend, I have found the way to cross this bridge, and I sincerely want to help you cross it too. I want you to get out of the miserable, painful life you're living and help you begin a new life—a life full of joy, fulfillment, and excitement. But before I can do that, the question I must ask you is, how desperate are you? Are you desperate for a change in your life? If you're no longer content to stay where you are, to keep living the way you have been living, then there is help and hope for you.

Crossing over the bridge takes faith, courage, and determination. If you're not desperate for change, it is easy to turn away and to try to find an easier route to happiness. But if you've had enough of all the pain and disappointments, and you're willing to do whatever it takes to cross over the bridge, then please keep reading. I want to tell you about my journey, and how I discovered this bridge. I want to show you how to find it and cross it. Most of all, I want you to experience the amazing life that is waiting for you on the other side.

I'm a problem solver by nature. When something isn't working, I need to figure out a way to fix it. I was desperate and determined to be joyful, no matter what my circumstances, because the Bible said I could be. I was sick and tired of feeling depressed and hopeless, but the simple answers I had been given from others never seemed to work in my life. I needed a strategy, a plan, or a method that I could follow every time I felt trapped in sadness or anxiety. I cried out to God. I asked Him to help me find a way that would work for me and He answered my prayer. That is how I learned to cross over the bridge.

They say people teach what they need to learn. Well, this is something that I have needed to learn throughout my life, and I'm sure I will need to continue learning it. I don't ever want to stop learning and growing. The insights in this book aren't new, but their application has been a life-changing revelation to me. The Lord has shown me the way to have a life worth living, and I want to share it with you. My hope is that you will experience the freedom and joy that I have found.

I have found that the first step on this journey, this bridge, is the hardest. Don't let that stop you or discourage you. Press on! The second step is a challenge also. However, each step progressively becomes easier, and the power, sense of accomplishment, joy, and excitement you will experience will spur you on to the end. You can cross this bridge and discover your greatest joy, even in the middle of your darkest night, if you persevere. I know you can do it! I hope you will keep reading and allow me the privilege of sharing my discovery with you.

Make it personal:

1. Do you experience joy in all circumstances? Why, or why not?

2. What usually makes you feel happy?

3. In the past, what has robbed you of joy?

4. Do you believe it is possible to always be joyful? Why, or why not?

CHAPTER ONE

Searching for Joy

I've always envied happy people. They can walk into a room and light it up with their smile. They seem to possess a natural sense of humor and a contagious, positive outlook on life. They're fun to be with and can create a party atmosphere wherever they go, no matter who is there.

I've had the privilege of knowing several people like that. In fact, my husband and some of my best friends belong to that "happy people" club. They have the ability to bring happiness into my life, even when I don't feel like being happy. But I know they're in my life for another reason—to show me that I can *be* one of those people, not by becoming momentarily happy, but by experiencing constant joy.

Joy has not come naturally to me. I wasn't born with a cheerful personality, so I've had to work at it. I've had a lifetime of difficult challenges, and each one brought with it the potential for stealing my joy.

All Things Work for Good

The first time I heard the words "all things work together for good," I was fifteen years old and a young man had crushed my heart. A well-meaning Christian friend assured me that God would somehow use my pain for good in my life, but I couldn't see how any good could come from the feelings of betrayal and rejection that I was dealing with. I was angry. Why would a loving God allow a young girl to be treated so unfairly? He could have prevented me from meeting that young man and saved me from the pain.

But every day I thought about those words. They come from a verse in the Bible: "And we know that God causes everything to work together for the good of those who love God and are called according to his purpose for them" (Romans 8:28, NLT). I rehearsed them again and again, until I had committed them to memory. I started to believe them. I realized that if I would make a decision to love God and surrender to His purpose for my life, He would somehow take my pain and make everything work out. I gave my life to Christ, and immediately, I experienced a joy in my soul like I had never known before.

Within a week, I was amazed to find that the heartache was completely gone. I felt empowered and excited about my new relationship with Christ. I had no idea at the time how powerful those few words from the Bible really were, and how much I would come to love them in the coming years.

Sadly, two months later, it seemed I had completely forgotten them. My father was a minister, and he accepted a position at a church in California. We moved halfway across the country. I left behind my friends, all of my older siblings, my nieces and nephews, my school and my church.

I arrived in California with intense loneliness and depression. For several weeks, I mourned, refusing to accept my fate. I was angry with God and sure that I would never be happy again. It seemed that the brief joy I had experienced had disappeared.

There were a few moments during this time of teenage trauma when I considered suicide, but fortunately, my dislike for pain prevented me from pursuing it. I tried desperately to convince my parents that I should move back to Colorado and live with my older sister, but they could not be persuaded.

One night, long after everyone else was asleep, I lay in my bed sobbing. Feeling misunderstood, completely alone, and doomed to a life of isolation, I turned back to God and begged Him for help. Jesus comforted me that night in my bedroom, and what I experienced was amazing. I didn't hear an audible voice, but I could hear Him speaking to me in my mind. It was incredible! I had never heard Him speak to me so clearly before. He reminded me of Romans 8:28. He assured me that He loved me, He was with me, and He had a perfect plan for me. I was overwhelmed with an indescribable joy.

He didn't change my circumstances, and I still wasn't happy about them, but that night, He healed my heart. I cried out to Him, and He answered me! The God of the universe spoke to me! If He loved me enough to do that, then I believed that what He said was true. I knew He had a plan for my life, and everything was going to work out for the best.

My new outlook gave me an opportunity to develop relationships with some of the Christians at my high school, and they led me to an exciting, Spirit-filled church. I started attending it regularly and experienced a sweet sense of joy each time I went. I was learning a lot about the Bible and growing in my relationship with Jesus. It was wonderful!

Nevertheless, too many of my days were still filled with sadness or anger. In my Bible, I read 1 Thessalonians 5:16. It said we should always be joyful. I wanted to feel joy all the time, but how? How could someone possibly be "joyful always"?

Pursuing His Presence

My high school years were full of emotional ups and downs, but when it ended, I was left with nothing but "downs." Most of my friends left town to attend college, and I was incredibly lonely and depressed—again. My parents convinced me to enroll in a community college, but the demands were too overwhelming and I dropped out during my second semester. I was empty and searching for something to fill the void in my life. I knew God was near, but I couldn't sense His presence anymore.

Deuteronomy 4:29 (NIV) says, "But if from there you seek the Lord your God, you will find Him if you look for Him with all your heart and with all your soul." I was searching for God's presence in my life without understanding the big "ifs" in that verse. I wanted God to meet my needs and fill my emptiness, but I wasn't ready to surrender to *His* way of doing that. So I used my own.

My loneliness and depression led me down a path of unhealthy relationships and ended in a marriage filled with abuse, infidelity, two babies, and finally a divorce. My way had failed. Stripped of my pride and selfishness and desperate to survive for the sake of our two beautiful little girls, I surrendered to God's ways once more. I cried out to Him, and He answered me.

Psalm 34:18 (NIV) says, "The Lord is close to the brokenhearted, and saves those who are crushed in spirit." As a single mother, I faced tremendous obstacles nearly every day, but God's presence was so near I felt I could almost touch Him. I had an amazing sense of peace and strength. I spent hours each evening singing praise songs, reading my Bible, praying and reciting scriptures. God's love sustained me. I knew He was all I really needed and I could completely trust Him. When I was in His presence, nothing else mattered.

While I recognized His love was never changing, and I cherished the intimacy I experienced with Jesus, my joy still seemed to be inconsistent. I went back to school, but the pressure of being a mother of two preschoolers while attending college full time was so intense. My income alone was never enough to pay the bills, and although God miraculously provided for us every month, too often I cried myself to sleep at night. I was so thankful for His help and provision, and I really wanted to be happy all the time. I just didn't know how. I began to wonder if I was doomed to a life of depression, in spite of my relationship with Jesus.

I was determined to find the answer, so I spent time talking to God in prayer and studying His Word diligently. I learned a lot and had many days of breakthrough, but I wasn't satisfied with just a day of joy here and there. I wanted to "consider it *all* joy" (see James 1:2).

God heard my cries, and three years later, He did what He is so great at doing. In order to answer my prayers, He gave me what He knew I needed. He knew what would change me, and what would teach me about joy, but it was not what I had asked for or what I expected. I asked God to give me joy, and He gave me another husband and two stepchildren.

Roadblocks to Joy

My darling husband, Mark, and my wonderful stepchildren are three of the greatest gifts God has ever given me. They have filled my life with joy and blessings too numerous to count. But my relationship with them hasn't always been joyful. As a matter of fact, the first few years were actually more stressful, than joyful.

Most of us know that marriage can be difficult—no matter how wonderfully God-ordained the union is. But when you add four children to the mix, it can become overwhelming, and I was definitely overwhelmed. I was not at all prepared for the conflicts and rejection I received from my new stepchildren or the territorial battles between the new stepsiblings. Perhaps the biggest shock of all was the strife and division I experienced with my husband over some seemingly minor issues concerning our children.

As I said before, whenever I detect a problem, my initial impulse is to figure out how to solve it. So whenever I perceived a problem in our marriage, I set out to fix it. And usually that meant Mark had to change something in order for the problem to be solved. I would pray for him, but with my own goals and desires in mind, rather than asking God to fulfill His will in our lives.

During the early years of our marriage, I didn't really respect Mark for the way God had made him. I didn't like the way he treated my children, I didn't like the way he treated his children, and I didn't like the way he treated me. I wanted him to be what I wanted him to be, and I thought that God wanted him to be that way too. So I tried to help God out by trying to get Mark to change.

After a few years of this, Mark began to get very weary of hearing about the things that he needed to change. He started to withdraw from me, and our relationship became more and more difficult.

At first, this made me so frustrated that I became more determined than ever to correct the problems. But the hurt, rejection, and isolation I was feeling caused me to eventually give up and withdraw from him as well. Our relationship grew cold. We lived almost completely separate lives, speaking only when it concerned the children or our finances, but rarely discussing anything else, and rarely being intimate with each other. Our purpose for staying together became simply about caring for the children

Because we were having marital problems, we started withdrawing from our family and friends. We were too embarrassed to discuss our problems with people from our church. We didn't know any other couples that had a blended family or could relate to our issues. But the more isolated we became, the easier it became to think about giving up and just getting a divorce. After all, who would know, and who would even care?

This pattern continued for years. I was depressed a lot of the time and very lonely. Once again I felt angry and abandoned by God. How could He have allowed me to commit myself to something so unrewarding and hurtful? I was miserable. I cried a lot, whined a lot, and tried every method I could think of to change the people around me. I was sure they were the ones responsible for my misery.

When that didn't seem to work, I decided that the only way I was going to find happiness was to get out of the marriage. I planned my escape and figured out my future. I knew in my heart that I was rebelling against God, but I didn't care. I just wanted an end to my pain. I made temporary arrangements for my children and left.

I found a brief relief, perhaps like the sensation you feel immediately after a splinter has been removed from your finger. But the wound was much deeper than I had realized, and as the days passed, my heart began to ache for God's presence. I wanted out of my marriage, but I had no intention of turning away from my God. Yet I felt like He had left me. I couldn't hear His voice anymore or sense His love. My spirit was sick, and the peace I used to know had vanished. My body responded with fatigue, nausea, and even occasional vomiting. I cried and prayed, but God was silent. This time, He didn't rescue me or heal me. My wounds had become infected with sin and were oozing the repulsive puss of rebellion.

First Samuel 15:23 (NLT) says, "Rebellion is as sinful as witchcraft, and stubbornness as bad as worshiping idols." Rebellion against God's Word is a direct refusal to let Him be in charge. When we insist on having our way, we are making a choice to be our own god. We are rejecting God with a false sense of pride. First Peter 5:5b (NLT) tells us that "God opposes the proud, but gives grace to the humble." When we are full of pride, God actually works against us, until we recognize that He is God and His ways are best. For a great illustration of this, read chapters 38–42 in the book of Job. God will always love us. Nothing will ever separate us from His love, but sin and rebellion will separate us from His blessings.

For days, I tried to ignore the emptiness I felt inside, but the more I attempted to fill my life with worldly pleasures, the greater the void became. I had known the indescribable joy of experiencing God's love and presence, and nothing this life had to offer could compare. I couldn't eat or sleep. I was broken, and I didn't know what to do. I sank into a deep depression and began to sob uncontrollably.

Then God spoke. I heard His voice in my head so clearly that it was almost audible. He said, "Go home." That wasn't what I wanted to hear, not at all. I wanted Him to tell me He loved me and that everything was going to be all right. I wanted

Him to tell me that He was going to fix my life and make me happy again. I argued with God as I cried, insisting that things were never going to change and I would always be miserable if I went back home. But He said it again, "Go home." I knew I didn't have a choice. I either had to surrender to Him, or lose my close relationship with Him.

Joy in Surrender

I lay on the bed all afternoon, crying and mourning the death of my plans and dreams. Then suddenly He spoke again, and what He said changed my life forever. He said, "If you leave this marriage, you will be leaving more than Mark and his children, you will be leaving ME. You will be leaving the things I have called you to do and the blessings I have prepared for you."

Something inside of me broke. I was grateful that God was speaking to me again. I needed to hear His voice. But I knew that what He was saying to me was true, and it was a painful revelation. Then the Lord said, "If Mark never changes, will you still obey Me? Or will you insist on having things your way?" I was so ashamed and heartbroken. I couldn't even utter an answer.

Then He said, "You need to put your desires on the altar. YOU need to lay yourself down on the altar and die. Then I can resurrect you and make YOU new." Initially, those words were devastating. I felt like God was turning against me. But I had no choice because I knew I could never walk away from my God. So that afternoon, the bed became an altar. I fell down across the bed, weeping, letting the old me die, and surrendering all of my needs and desires.

Psalm 30:5 (NLT) says, "For His anger lasts only a moment, but His favor lasts a lifetime! Weeping may last through the night, but joy comes with the morning."

I surrendered that day, humbled and broken. But just moments later, God spoke again. What He showed me instantly changed my perspective and healed my broken heart.

I love what The Message Bible says in Luke 6:21, "You're blessed when the tears flow freely. Joy comes with the morning." Jeremiah 31:13b (NIV) says, "I will turn their mourning into gladness; I will give them comfort and joy instead of sorrow." He literally turned my mourning into gladness. I had a revelation that day that turned me into a completely different person.

Through my sorrow, God revealed the things that had kept me from experiencing His joy continuously, and He gave me the tools I needed to remove those obstacles. That revelation has continued to sustain me through every tragedy and trial I have ever had to face, and there have been many. I am writing this book to share that revelation so that others who struggle as I did can experience everlasting, indescribable joy.

I went home the next day with a new commitment to my marriage, but more importantly, with a new commitment to my Lord. I discovered that joy, outside of His will for my life, was not joy at all, but only momentary happiness that could easily be snatched away with any unpleasant circumstance. Joy, true joy, had risen out of the ashes of surrender. I knew it was going to be possible, with God's help, to "always be full of joy in the Lord" (Philippians 4:4).

Joy in Suffering

I think it is natural for us as humans to attempt to find happiness by avoiding suffering. But joy, lasting joy, actually comes to us by going *through* suffering. Once we have experienced loss and heartache, we can better appreciate our blessings and the joy that they bring.

A few years after my decision to surrender to God's will and commit to my marriage, my determination to "always be full of joy" was severely tested. My daughter Ashley, who was seventeen at the time, and my stepdaughter Aimee, who was fourteen, were driving home from church on a Sunday morning. A young woman ran through a red light and hit Ashley's car. Ashley was killed instantly, and Aimee was seriously injured.

I was out of town when it happened. I received a phone call about the accident, but I wasn't given any of the details. I was just told to hurry home. My mind began to race as I imagined all the different scenarios. I feared that one or both of our daughters had been killed. I had a four-hour drive home and during that ride God and I had a conversation.

The first thing I cried was, "NO! I can't do this, Lord! I told you that I would do anything for you, but not this! I can't do this!"

And the Lord softly and gently said, "Yes, you can. You can do all things through Christ."

I sobbed, "But, Lord, those are my children!!"

And God sweetly said, "I know exactly how you feel. I watched my Son die too."

During that long drive home, I listened to worship music. God kept speaking, encouraging me to trust Him. Miraculously, I was able to drive without tears. I began to see that He truly understood my pain. He knew what I was going through. And He was going to use this somehow to bring glory to His name and bring more people to Him. I think my body was in shock. But my spirit was unusually strong. Somehow, I surrendered to God's will for me, no matter what it was.

As soon as I did that, my demeanor and thoughts completely changed. There was an amazing grace for the journey and a strength that I had never experienced before. The warrior inside me was ready to fight. I was serving as a children's pastor at that time, and I saw this as a direct attack from Satan to stop the work that I was doing with children. So I made a vow that I would not let the devil win. Whatever happened was not going to stop me. It was only going to make me stronger and I was more determined than ever to bring people into God's family, just to spite the devil.

When I made it home and found out that my stepdaughter was in the hospital and that my daughter was dead, I was devastated. But that week, as I made the arrangements for her memorial service, I had an amazing sense of God's presence, a supernatural feeling of peace and strength. Every time I broke down in sorrow, the Lord would speak to me and comfort me with exactly what I needed to hear.

Ashley had a passionate love for Jesus, and He reminded me that she was in heaven with Him. He surrounded me with incredible people to take care of every detail of my life. They provided my family and me with meals, cards, gifts, flowers, clean laundry, and a clean house. They helped us plan a beautiful memorial service and video. God was showering me with His love and care.

I went through a very difficult time of grief for several months after Ashley's death. The pain of such a devastating loss is indescribable. But my sorrow caused me to spend hours every day just listening to God's voice and feeding my spirit with spiritual songs and with His Word. I could sense His presence, comfort, and strength. I felt His peace and joy in the midst of my pain.

When my initial stage of grieving came to an end, I had more zeal and passion for child evangelism than I had ever experienced before. Since my daughter had died at a young age, I realized how critical it was for children to know Jesus personally, as soon as they were old enough to understand the Gospel message. During the next ten years that I served as a children's pastor, I had the privilege of leading over four hundred children and about thirty-five adults to Christ.

The year Ashley died, she had written a letter to God on New Year's Eve. She asked God to use her as a tool to save others. Fourteen young people gave their lives to Christ at Ashley's memorial service. In the years following her death, I heard dozens of reports of young people making decisions for Christ as her youth pastor and others would share with them the story of her sudden death. God has used her death to reach hundreds of people.

My own relationship with Jesus deepened after Ashley's death as well. He became so real and close to me, and I can honestly say that I know I love Him more than anything in this world. What could have made me bitter only made me love Him more! I'm so thankful that I had learned how to surrender to His will through the previous struggles in my marriage. In His merciful, loving way, my Father God prepared me for the pain of losing my first-born child.

Two years after her death, I had a vision of heaven. I saw myself entering and Jesus was there, waiting for me with His arms wide open. He took me in his arms and we began to dance. I noticed that there was a circle of people all around us and they were watching and smiling as we danced. Out of the corner of my eye, I could see the people in the circle. I saw my grandparents, my parents, two of my brothers, and I saw Ashley. But I was so taken with Jesus and so thrilled to be with Him that I couldn't take my eyes off of Him. I didn't run to Ashley like I thought I would. Jesus had become more important to me than my own daughter! And then He said to me, "You see, you really do love me more than anything else in the world and I am so pleased with you."

My whole perspective on this world has changed because of what I went through. As much as I miss my daughter, I am thrilled that her death has meant salvation for hundreds of others, and I would never want to change that. I know I will see her again!

Oftentimes when tragedy strikes we try to figure out why it happened, to make some sense of it, but usually we can't. I think that's because we think too small! God is so much bigger and His ways are so much greater than ours. We see a tiny speck of what is happening, and we think of it as a tragedy. But what appears to be a tragedy may bring hundreds to Jesus, as Ashley's death did, and as Jesus's death did.

Isaiah 55:8, 9 (NLT) says, "My thoughts are nothing like your thoughts," says the Lord. "And my ways are far beyond anything you could imagine. For just as the heavens are higher than the earth, so my ways are higher than your ways and my thoughts higher than your thoughts."

A good father will choose to do what it best for his whole family. If that means that one of his children must be disciplined or deprived of something they really want, he will do it, if he believes that is what is best for the entire family. He won't sacrifice one of his children just to make another one happy.

God loves His children even more than an earthly father loves his children. Our loving Heavenly Father is busy doing what He needs to do to save *everyone*. He loves all of us! Nothing can separate us from His love! He knows that our suffering in this world is only temporary. He knows that we really can do all things through Christ who strengthens us, and He works everything together for good when we love Him in return!

These Bible verses encourage me daily:

"Yet what we suffer now is nothing compared to the glory he will reveal to us later." (Romans 8:18, NLT)

"Now we see things imperfectly, like puzzling reflections in a mirror, but then we will see everything with perfect clarity. All that I know now is partial and incomplete, but then I will know everything completely, just as God now knows me completely." (1 Corinthians 13:12, NLT)

"For our present troubles are small and won't last very long. Yet they produce for us a glory that vastly outweighs them and will last forever! So we don't look at the troubles we can see now; rather, we fix our gaze on things that cannot be seen. For the things we see now will soon be gone, but the things we cannot see will last forever." (2 Corinthians 4:17–18, NLT)

Without the Holy Spirit, we can only see a small part of what is happening in this world. It's similar to looking at the backside of a tapestry. It doesn't make much sense to us and it certainly doesn't look pretty. But after we learn to trust God and listen to His voice, we begin to see and understand more. We see that God is weaving all of our hurt and suffering into a beautiful tapestry.

When God reveals things to us that are happening in the spiritual realm, we still can only see a part of what He is doing. Our minds can't comprehend all that God knows and sees. But one day we *will* understand, and we will see the beautiful picture that God sees.

Joy in Obedience

After my daughter's death, I realized that *my* time on this earth was short as well, and I needed to live every day as though it were my last, driven only by the things that mattered for eternity. That attitude gave me the courage to obey whatever the Lord told me to do and experience all kinds of exciting and miraculous adventures, things I might never have considered doing before.

Four years after her death, my husband and I answered the call to become foster parents. We opened our home to three siblings, who were three, five, and seven years old. It was extremely stressful and overwhelming at times, but it also brought tremendous joy into our home.

After fostering for almost three years, the Lord called us to adopt them, and although we were somewhat fearful of the huge task and responsibility, we agreed to start the process. As soon as we agreed, we entered into a fierce spiritual and legal battle, but once again, God provided us with the strength, faith, and courage we needed to persevere. When the adoption was finalized, there was a lot of rejoicing and celebration in our home.

A year later, we felt the Lord had called us to leave our positions of employment at our church and move to Colorado to work in ministry there. After much prayer and counsel, we stepped out in faith and resigned, only to experience ten months of unemployment while we waited for our house to sell. We wondered if we had misunderstood what God had told us to do. When our savings account was almost depleted, we started to look for work and took our house off the market.

The week before we spent our last dollar, we were asked to move to Colorado, all expenses paid, and join the staff of a large church near Denver. That same week, we were offered our asking price for our home, even though it had been taken off of the market! It was a challenging and amazing experience, to say the least. But God blessed our obedience beyond our wildest dreams and there were many moments of incredible joy.

Joy Always

I have experienced God's peace, joy, love and faithfulness in the midst of difficult circumstances countless times in my life, but not every time, and certainly not all the time. My life has not been easy. Not at all! At different times in my life, I have suffered with chronic pain, depression, rejection, loneliness, betrayal, unemployment, financial losses, aging parents, fear, anxiety, anger, death, divorce, confusion, sickness, disappointment, and much heartbreak. If I were to tell you about all my experiences, I would probably need to write several more books.

But the point of this book is not to tell you about all the problems I have had or the blessings I have enjoyed. I have had my share of both. In our society, we are expected to be joyful during the good times, and it is generally accepted that sadness and even depression are a normal part of life as well, particularly if things aren't going well. But the Bible teaches that we should rejoice always (Philippians 4:4), and always be joyful (1 Thessalonians 5:16). How is that even possible?

Finding the answer to that question has been a life-long journey for me. Each time I faced a challenge, I learned a lesson. Sometimes I was a quick learner. Other times, it took me awhile to catch on. I have discovered that it *is* possible to experience the joy of the Lord always, and now I will never be the same. If I had known before what I know now, I believe all my difficult circumstances would have been much easier for me to endure. My hope and prayer is that I can share with you what I have learned from my experiences, and that you too will be able to rejoice always.

Make it personal:

1. Has there ever been a time in your life when you felt hurt or abandoned by God?

2. In the past, how have you responded to difficult circumstances?

3. What were the consequences of your responses?

4. Have you learned and/or changed from your past experiences?

5. If so, in what ways?

6. Is there anything you wish you had done differently?

CHAPTER TWO

A Shocking Revelation

Exposing the Obstacles to Joy

I'm sure you have heard someone say that joy is a choice. I can say that I agree with that statement now. But that wasn't always the case. As I have shared, I struggled for decades to become a joyful person, even though I genuinely tried to "choose" joy. I knew that simply saying that you're going to be joyful, or choosing to act joyfully, is not the same as actually *feeling* joyful. What I really wanted was to *feel* joyful!

The Bible is full of passages that exhort us to be joyful, so I think joy is a big deal to God. Jesus said that we could be filled with joy, overflowing joy! (See John 15:11 and 17:13.) Paul said that our joy proves that the Holy Spirit is in us (Galatians 5:22) and that we should always be full of joy (Phil. 4:4). The book of James tells us that trouble is actually an opportunity for joy (James 1:2). Peter says we should rejoice when we are suffering (1 Peter 4:13). The prophet Nehemiah told the people, "The joy of the Lord is your strength" (Nehemiah 8:10).

If we don't have joy, then we are weak. Joy is important to God, not just because He loves us and wants us to be happy, but because it enables us to stand strong against our enemy, the devil. We need to be strong if we are going to accomplish anything for the Kingdom of God, so we *need* the joy of the Lord. How can we be a positive witness for Christ if we are miserable all the time? Why would anyone want to sign up for that?

In the past, I truly wanted to be a strong Christian, to be a good witness for God, and to do great things for Him. But I knew my frequent tendency to slip into depression was keeping me from being everything God wanted me to be. After years of pretending to be happy, while feeling miserable inside, I became desperate. I needed to figure out the key to experiencing the joy of the Lord all the time. I needed to know how people did that. Why did it seem so easy for some and such a struggle for others like me?

When I left my husband, I experienced one of the darkest times of my life. I cried out to God and begged Him to show me what to do. He answered me, but I didn't like His answer. He repeated His answer again, and then He waited. He didn't say anything else to me, until I was ready to surrender to His will.

I let go of my dreams and my plans that day, surrendered to God's plan for me, and as soon as I did, my spiritual eyes were opened. He showed me what would happen if I continued my rebellion. For the first time, I was aware of the harmful patterns in my life. He asked me some questions about my past. When was it easy for me to be joyful? When was it difficult? When I felt unhappy, what were the obstacles that prevented my joy?

As I thought about the answers to those questions, I began to see the patterns emerging. There were two very obvious things that prevented my joy, over and over again. They were (1) imperfect circumstances and (2) imperfect people. Basically, that meant that the only times I had been joyful, were the times when I thought everything was perfect. Ouch!

The Greatest Commandment

That day, I realized I had a lot of growing up to do if I was going to be like Christ. The Holy Spirit began to speak to me through God's Word. He brought these Scriptures to my mind:

> "And they overcame him because of the blood of the Lamb and because of the word of their testimony, and they did not love their life even when faced with death." (Rev. 12:11, NASB)
>
> "Then he said to the crowd, "If any of you wants to be my follower, you must give up your own way, take up your cross daily, and

follow me. If you try to hang on to your life, you will lose it. But if you give up your life for my sake, you will save it." (Luke 9:23–24, NLT)

"I tell you the truth, unless a kernel of wheat is planted in the soil and dies, it remains alone. But its death will produce many new kernels—a plentiful harvest of new lives." (John 12:24, NLT)

The Lord began to show me that if I would allow myself to "die," He would raise me up, and I could become a different person—a person that He could use for His Kingdom, a person who would produce many seeds! In that moment, I knew that the only way to experience the joy of the Lord was to put God first. I had to start loving God more than anything else, even myself, and commit to obeying His Word, even when I didn't feel like doing it. There is no real joy outside of God's will. If I wanted to be in His will, I had to stop complaining and criticizing when things didn't go my way. I needed to choose to worship Him, trust Him, and thank Him, in *all* circumstances.

Matthew 22:34–40 (NLT) says,
"But when the Pharisees heard that he had silenced the Sadducees with his reply, they met together to question him again. One of them, an expert in religious law, tried to trap him with this question: 'Teacher, which is the most important commandment in the law of Moses?' Jesus replied, 'You must love the Lord your God with all your heart, all your soul, and all your mind.' This is the first and greatest commandment. A second is equally important: 'Love your neighbor as yourself.' The entire law and all the demands of the prophets are based on these two commandments."

In John 14:21–24 (NLT) Jesus said,

"'Those who accept my commandments and obey them are the ones who love me. And because they love me, my Father will love them. And I will love them and reveal myself to each of them.'" Judas (not Judas Iscariot, but the other disciple with that name) said to him, 'Lord, why are you going to reveal yourself only to us and not to the world at large?' Jesus replied, 'All who love me will do what I say. My Father will love them, and we will come and make our home with each of them. Anyone who doesn't love me will not obey me. And remember, my words are not my own. What I am telling you is from the Father who sent me.'"

Loving God is not just a warm fuzzy feeling. Jesus told us that we show our love for God through our obedience. He said, "When you obey my commandments, you remain in my love, just as I obey my Father's commandments and remain in his love. I have told you these things so that you will be filled with my joy. Yes, your joy will overflow! This is my commandment: Love each other in the same way I have loved you" (John 15:10–12, NLT). We obey God by loving Him and loving others. That is what brings us joy!

Jesus told us many things so that we could be filled with His joy (John 17:13). When we obey the Greatest Commandment (Matthew 22:34–40), we experience a miraculous joy that doesn't come from our circumstances. It comes from God! It is a gift to us! It is a reward and blessing for simply doing what God has told us to do.

God showed me that my husband would never be able to meet all my needs, and he wasn't supposed to. Only God can do that. God wanted us to enjoy our marriage. But more importantly, He brought us together so that we could fulfill His plan for our lives. Mark and I would only experience true joy and fulfillment when we focused on God's plans and desires for us, rather than our own. I needed to let go of all my expectations. My desires for romance, for conversation, for control, for appreciation—everything I wanted couldn't be more important to me than what God wanted for me. Those things that I thought I needed were becoming idols, and they needed to be removed.

When we focus on our own needs, or even on someone else's needs, it is so easy to let our emotions dictate our actions. For example, if my husband treats me well, then I find it easy to treat him well. But if I'm upset with my husband, then I have a hard time caring about his needs.

However, if my focus is completely on pleasing the Lord, then the way someone else behaves is really insignificant. I can choose to do what is right out of my love for Jesus and my desire to obey Him. This applies to all our other relationships as well. His Word tells us how we are to treat others. We are to love them as we love ourselves.

We can love our spouse best when we love God most. My marriage has a much greater purpose than just providing me with a lover, helper, companion, and father for my children. God wants to bless Christian marriages so they will advance His Kingdom! He wants them to be used for ministry.

Ruth Bell Graham said, "It is a foolish woman who expects her husband to be to her that which only Jesus Christ Himself can be: ready to forgive, totally understanding, unendingly patient, invariably tender and loving, unfailing in every area, anticipating every need, and making more than adequate provision. Such expectations put a man under an impossible strain."[1] I believe the same goes for the man who expects too much from his wife. Only Jesus can meet our every need.

The Key to Joy

I discovered that the key to finding joy was not in trying to be joyful or pursuing joy at all. The key to experiencing joy was *giving love*! *Loving* fills us with joy! "Beloved, let us love one another, for love is from God; and everyone who loves is born of God and knows God. The one who does not love does not know God, for God is love" (1 John 4:7, 8, NASB).

We can't experience joy apart from experiencing love! We may be able to find temporary happiness when we focus on our own needs and desires. But the only way to know the indescribable joy of the Lord is to lay down our lives for God and for others; to love them the way Christ loves us. Unconditionally.

This truth definitely applies to marriage, but it also applies to every other relationship in our lives. Jesus said we are to love everyone, even our enemies! (Matthew 5:44, Luke 6:27). He also said, "Your enemies will be right in your own household!" (Matthew 10:36, NLT).

Sometimes the person in your life who is the hardest to love lives under the very same roof. It could be a sibling, a parent, a stepsibling or stepparent, an in-law, or a roommate. The biological connection makes no difference. Living with someone can be difficult under the best of circumstances. Living with someone that we constantly disagree with, or someone who has been habitually hurtful and selfish can be unbearable.

Is it impossible to love someone we don't like? Without God's help, I would have to say, yes. But nothing is impossible with God (Luke 1:37). If we truly love God, and we want to experience a life filled with joy, then we need to obey His command to love everyone, even the people we want to hate.

I appreciate the way The Message Bible has translated 1 Timothy 1:5. It says, "The whole point of what we're urging is simply love—love uncontaminated by self-interest and counterfeit faith, a life open to God." Love is the whole point of the Gospel and love is the whole point of living for God.

First Corinthians 13:2 says that without love, we are nothing. Chapter 13 of 1 Corinthians is sometimes referred to as the love chapter. When you read these verses, you can't ignore the importance of love in the life of a Christian.

> "If I could speak all the languages of earth and of angels, but didn't love others, I would only be a noisy gong or a clanging cymbal. If I had the gift of prophecy, and if I understood all of God's secret plans and possessed all knowledge, and if I had such faith that I could move mountains, but didn't love others, I

would be nothing. If I gave everything I have to the poor and even
sacrificed my body, I could boast
about it; but if I didn't love others,
I would have gained nothing.

"Love is patient and kind.
Love is not jealous or boastful or
proud or rude. It does not demand
its own way. It is not irritable,
and it keeps no record of being
wronged. It does not rejoice about
injustice but rejoices whenever the
truth wins out. Love never gives up,
never loses faith, is always hope-
ful, and endures through every
circumstance.

"Prophecy and speaking in
unknown languages and special
knowledge will become useless.
But love will last forever! Now our
knowledge is partial and incomplete, and even the gift of prophecy
reveals only part of the whole picture! But when the time of perfec-

tion comes, these partial things will become useless.

"When I was a child, I spoke and thought and reasoned as a child. But when I grew up, I put away childish things. Now we see things imperfectly, like puzzling reflections in a mirror, but then we will see everything with perfect clarity. All that I know now is partial and incomplete, but then I will know everything completely, just as God now knows me completely.

"Three things will last forever—faith, hope, and love—and the greatest of these is love." (1 Corinthians 13:1–13, NLT)

To be perfectly transparent, I have struggled to love others most of my life, which explains why I struggled to find joy most of my life. First, I struggled to love my older brother, who teased me throughout my childhood and adolescence. Then, I struggled to love my first husband, who eventually became unfaithful and abusive. (Just a side note. I do *not* condone abuse of any kind. Some people must be loved from afar, for our own safety).

There were times when I struggled to love my employer, co-workers, my staff, or my relatives. Sometimes I struggled to love my second husband and my stepchildren. When I was serving as a teacher, a minister, and a foster parent, there were times I had to deal with difficult people, and I struggled to love them as well. I was even challenged at times to love my own teenagers, when they were acting defiant, selfish, or rude.

Yes, I have struggled. Love isn't easy. In fact, true love, the kind we read about in 1 Corinthians 13, is hard! But when I learned *how* to love someone who is difficult to love, it became so much easier. I became free of the bondage of anger and hate and I learned to experience joy, no matter who was in my life.

I'm a little past middle age now, and as I've gotten older, my body has more physical aches and pains, especially after a day of manual labor. But because I have learned to love, my mind is at peace, my heart is happy, and it is well with my soul.

When I was younger, my body was strong and limber. I could work all day without pain. But my mind was often anxious, my heart was heavy, and my soul was restless. I can honestly say, I would much rather be older, with a weaker body and a joyful heart, than to be young again with a strong body and a sad heart.

If you are unhappy, depressed, anxious, or angry, take inventory of all the people in your life. I can almost guarantee that you will think of someone you don't love, and maybe even someone that you hate. Examine your relationship with Jesus as well. Do you love Him more than anything else in your life?

If you realize that there is someone in your life that you don't love, or if you're not sure if you really love Jesus, don't be discouraged. Don't let that worry you or stop you from pressing on and pursuing joy. God still loves you and He wants to bless you with joy. He has created a way for you to cross the bridge that leads to joy. He has a perfect plan, and it will enable you to walk across that bridge. It is the way that leads to love, the perfect love that only God can give. Love is the key to joy, and I know that you can cross the bridge that takes you to love! Please keep reading, and let me explain.

Make it personal:

1. Why does God want you to be joyful all the time?

2. Is there anything in your life that you love more than you love God?

3. According to John 14:21, how do we show God we love Him?

4. In John 15:10–12, what does Jesus say we will have as a result of our obedience?

5. Is there anyone in your life that you don't love?

6. What is the only way to know the indescribable joy of the Lord?

CHAPTER THREE

It's Easier Said Than Done

So all you need is love! Great! If love is the key to joy, then it should be simple to find joy, right? Wrong! As you probably know, love can be anything but easy.

We all have people in our lives that are ridiculously difficult to love, and I'm no exception. I know how to experience joy, but it is so much easier said than done. I wish I could say I operate in love all the time, but unfortunately, I can't. I have failed time and time again.

I'm a former teacher, foster parent, and pastor. Loving others has always been a very essential part of my career and my calling. But I had to learn how to love others. It did not come naturally or easily to me. I had to realize that the only way I could love another person unconditionally was with God's help. It is His Spirit inside of us that enables us to do that (2 Tim. 1:7). And if we want God's help, then we have to start by loving God.

One might assume that loving God would be an easy thing to do. After all, He is loving, forgiving, kind, and faithful to us. But 1 John 2:5 (NLT) says, "Those who obey God's Word truly show how completely they love Him." When we realize that loving God means obeying Him, we can easily see how we fall short of that as well. The one thing God wants from us more than anything else is our obedience. First Samuel 15:22 (NLT) makes that pretty clear. "What is more pleasing to the Lord: your burnt offerings and sacrifices, or your obedience to his voice? Listen! Obedience is better than sacrifice, and submission is better than offering the fat of rams."

In Galatians 5:22, the apostle Paul lists the fruit of the Spirit. When we are filled with the Holy Spirit, these things should be evident in our lives. They are love, joy, peace, patience, kindness, goodness, faithfulness, gentleness, and self-control. I believe they are purposefully listed in this order because love must come first. We cannot experience any of the other fruit in our lives, including joy, if we don't have love. In 1 Corinthians, chapter 13, Paul warns us that nothing we do for God will matter if we don't have love.

So if love is the key to joy, what do we do when we don't feel love toward someone? Jesus said we should love our enemies, but that can seem impossible! What do we do when we don't want to show love to God by obeying Him? Let's look at two men from the Bible who struggled with those thoughts and feelings and see how each of them responded.

Two Kings, Two Choices, Two Results

The first book of Samuel tells the stories of two kings, King Saul and King David.

Saul

Samuel was a prophet in the land of Israel during that time. When God's people, the Israelites, begged Samuel for a king, the Lord told His prophet Samuel to anoint Saul as king. But listen to Samuel's warning to the people in 1 Samuel 12:12–15 (NLT).

> "But when you were afraid of Nahash, the king of Ammon, you came to me and said that you wanted a king to reign over you, even though the Lord your God was already your king. All right, here is the king you have chosen. You asked for him, and the Lord has granted your request.
> "Now if you fear and worship the Lord and listen to his voice, and if you do not rebel against the Lord's commands, then both you and your king will show that you recognize the Lord as your God.

> But if you rebel against the Lord's commands and refuse to listen to him, then his hand will be as heavy upon you as it was upon your ancestors."

Samuel made it clear to the Israelites that there would be a consequence for any disobedience, whether by the people or the king. He told them that he would continue to teach them what was good and right, and that they must be careful to follow God's laws. Yet shortly after that, Saul disobeyed the instructions that Samuel gave him by offering a sacrifice himself. And when Samuel confronted his disobedience, Saul made an excuse for it.

We see this same pattern again in chapter 15. Samuel gave Saul instructions from the Lord. Saul was supposed to completely destroy the Amalekite nation, every single person and all the livestock. But Saul decided to spare the king's life, and he and his men kept the best of the livestock for themselves, and everything else that appealed to them. When Samuel confronted Saul about his disobedience, this time, Saul completely denied that he disobeyed. Then Samuel told him the consequence of his rebellion. Saul finally admitted that he had sinned, but by then it was too late. "Because you have rejected the command of the Lord, He has rejected you as king" (1 Samuel 15:23b, NLT).

David

Now let's look at King David. His story begins in 1 Samuel, chapter 16, and it ends in 1 Kings, chapter 2. I highly recommend you read all about him. His story is fascinating, and there are many lessons to be learned through his successes and his failures. God called David "a man after His own heart." David wrote many of the Psalms and the Lord rewarded him with a lasting dynasty. But David was far from perfect. He told lies, committed adultery, murder, and many other sins. Why did God favor David and bless him, but He rejected Saul? David's sins seem to be far worse than Saul's.

I believe there is one major reason God approved of David, yet rejected Saul. I believe the difference is so significant that it caused God to take the kingdom away from Saul and give it all to David, in spite of David's sins. God rewarded David with a lasting legacy and blessed his family for generations. If we want the Lord to bless our lives the way He blessed David's life, it's important that we understand what David did to receive such favor from the Lord.

As a young man, David served his family by caring for the sheep. He was a courageous, faithful, and dedicated shepherd. While Saul was still alive and reigning over Israel, the Lord told Samuel to go and anoint David to be the next king. David could have become prideful after that or tried to take matters into his own hands, but he did neither. He continued to serve as a shepherd.

Saul knew nothing about what Samuel had done. One day, he summoned David to work for him as a musician in his court. David left his family and faithfully served King Saul. Saul was very happy with him at first, and after David killed Goliath, Saul even promoted him to a commander in his army.

Things were going very well for David until Saul heard some of the Israelite women singing David's praises. Saul became extremely jealous and started to hate David. He demoted him and tried to kill him more than once. Eventually, David had to run away from Saul.

Saul became obsessed with killing David and tried to find him. But David still honored Saul as the king, and he never retaliated. He even spared Saul's life when he had opportunities to take it.

While David continued to run from Saul, he attracted an army of men. Eventually Saul died, and the people of Judah made David their king. But the Israelites chose Saul's son, Ishbosheth, to be the king of Israel. David had to wait seven more years before he finally became the king of Israel. He reigned over all Israel and Judah for thirty-three years.

During his reign, he had many victories, but he also made foolish mistakes, experienced loss, and caused needless suffering. One of the most notable problems he created was his relationship with Bathsheba, the wife of one of his soldiers. David summoned her and slept with her while her husband was away in battle. When she discovered she was pregnant, David made sure her husband was killed, so he could take her as his wife and hide his deeds. But when the Lord sent the prophet Nathan to confront David with his sin, David's reaction was pivotal, and we need to take note of it.

Second Samuel 12:13a (NLT) reads, "Then David confessed to Nathan, 'I have sinned against the Lord.'" David confessed. He admitted that what he did was wrong and that he had sinned against the Lord. Compare that with Saul's reaction when confronted by Samuel, and I think you can see a distinct difference. Saul made excuses for his sins or denied them altogether. But David confessed, and his relationship with God was restored.

Step One: Confess

When we examine the lives of these two kings, we can only conclude that admitting and confessing our sin must be a very important part of our relationship with God. It is the very first step we need to take whenever we have disobeyed God and we desire reconciliation. It is also the first step that leads us to salvation. Romans 10:9 says, "If you confess with your mouth that Jesus is Lord, and believe in your heart that God raised Him from the dead, you will be saved." We cannot have a relationship with the Father, unless we acknowledge that we have sinned and need Jesus to be our Lord and Savior.

Confession also plays an important role in our ability to experience joy. Look at 1 John 1:4–10 (NLT):

> "We are writing these things so that you may fully share our joy. This is the message we heard from Jesus and now declare to you: God is light, and there is no darkness in him at all. So we are lying if we say we have fellowship with God but go on living in spiritual darkness; we are not practicing the truth. But if we are living in the light, as God is in the light, then we have fellowship with each other, and the

blood of Jesus, his Son, cleanses us from all sin. If we claim we have no sin, we are only fooling ourselves and not living in the truth. But if we confess our sins to him, he is faithful and just to forgive us our sins and to cleanse us from all wickedness. If we claim we have not sinned, we are calling God a liar and showing that his word has no place in our hearts."

So if love is the key to joy, what do we do when we don't feel love toward someone? What do we do when we don't want to show our love for God by obeying Him? We admit it and *confess* it to God. When we bring our sin out into the open and expose it to God's light, we can have fellowship with God and with others.

This is the very first step across the bridge to a brand-new life. I know it can be extremely hard to do, but it is essential. We can't get across the bridge any other way. You can't skip this step or take a shortcut. If you want to know the everlasting love and joy that God has promised you, you must take the first step and confess your sin.

Jesus made a way for us to be completely free of the pain and the eternal consequence of our sin. He paid the price for our sin when He died on the cross in our place. Through Jesus, God provided a way for us to be forgiven and cleansed from all our sins. But if we deny that we have sinned, then Jesus's death was meaningless. It is as though He died for nothing. We can only receive forgiveness for something when we acknowledge that we have done it.

Since God is light, and there is no darkness in Him, we cannot have fellowship with God while we are hiding or denying our sin. Light cannot have fellowship with darkness. Our sin must be brought out into the light. Once it is exposed, it can be erased.

Imagine that your sin is like an old roll of undeveloped photography film, before the days of digital cameras and instant cameras. Back in those days, when the photography film was removed from a camera, it had to be kept in the dark or it would be ruined. If it were exposed to the light, the photographs would have been completely destroyed. When our sin is exposed, just like an old roll of film, it can be destroyed because it loses its power over us.

If you're too young to even know what I'm talking about here, then here's another example. Imagine that your sin is like a nasty old vampire. When he is exposed to daylight, he dies. This is what happens to our sin when we confess it. When we expose it, it can come in contact with God's light, and be completely erased. Once we confess it, our relationship with our Father is restored, and we can feel His love and His presence in our lives again. His spirit fills us, and we are able to love others, as well.

Every one of us has sinned and we all are in need of forgiveness (Romans 3:23, 1 John 1:10). When you recognize your own sin and understand how much God has forgiven you, it becomes easier to forgive others for their sins. Jesus said that everyone who sins is a slave of sin (John 8:34). Sin makes us feel miserable and keeps us in bondage to anger and hate. Confessing it sets us free.

Most of us have some understanding of what sin is and would probably agree that adultery, murder, and stealing are sins. But sometimes we don't recognize our own sin, because it isn't one that is listed in the Ten Commandments. That's when we need to refer back to The Greatest Commandment in Matthew 22:34–40. If we don't have joy, that is a good indication that either we aren't really loving God, by obeying His Word, or we aren't loving people. We need to confess that to God and ask Him to forgive us.

If you're still struggling with the idea of confession, I recommend that you read the fourth chapter from the book of James in the Bible. It sheds more light on the power of sin and the purpose of confession. James 4:6–7 (NLT) says, "God opposes the proud, but gives grace to the humble. So humble yourselves before God. Resist the devil and he will flee from you." Verse 10 says, "Humble yourselves before the Lord, and He will lift you up in honor." God stands against us when we are too proud to admit we were wrong. But when we are humble, God favors us and the devil loses his power over us!

Verse 17 says, "Remember, it is sin to know what you ought to do and then not do it." So sin can be defined as ignoring something God has told us to do, or just thinking that our way is better than God's way.

Do you have a tendency to complain or criticize? That is not pleasing to God, so confess it. Read Numbers 11:1, Philippians 2:14, and James 4:11. If you spend some time reading the New Testament, you will quickly become aware of the sin in your life. We all have failed to live up to the standards that Jesus set. I fail every day.

Are you frequently tempted to fear? When we have fear about any situation, or circumstance, or person, it is because we don't completely trust God. Fear destroys faith and Hebrews 11:6 tells us that it is impossible to please God without faith.

We are told not to fear at least 365 times in the Bible. That's one for every day of the year. God obviously wants us to live without fear. If we aren't following that commandment, then we need to admit it. Confessing is just admitting our faults or our weaknesses and acknowledging our need for God.

Are you constantly struggling with anger? Ephesians 4:26–27 (NLT) says, "Don't sin by letting anger control you. Don't let the sun go down while you are still angry, for anger gives a foothold to the devil." I have learned that unchecked anger can lead to many mental and physical illnesses.

When we are faced with the choice to remain angry, we must make a decision. With God's help, we can humble ourselves, forgive as we have been forgiven, and let it go. Or we can demand our rights, hold on to it and remain angry. If we choose to hold on to it, we are taking a step in the wrong direction and it will begin to control us, eventually leading us to sin and destruction.

Anger is a dark and dangerous hallway with many doors. The doors lead to hatred, rage, abuse, anxiety, depression, sickness, and pain. The longer we hold on to our anger, the further we walk down this hallway, opening doors and inviting more of the devil's influence and torment. The further we go, the more difficult it is to turn back. If you're struggling with anger, you can confess it right now and be rid of it. God is your avenger, and He is a just God. You can trust Him to defend you.

Romans 12:16–21 (NLT) says,

"Live in harmony with each other. Don't be too proud to enjoy the company of ordinary people. And don't think you know it all! Never pay back evil with more evil. Do things in such a way that everyone can see you are honorable. Do all that you can to live in peace with everyone. Dear friends, never take revenge. Leave that to the righteous anger of God. For the Scriptures say, "I will take revenge; I will pay them back," says the LORD. Instead, "If your enemies are hungry, feed them. If they are thirsty, give them something to drink. In doing this, you will heap burning coals of shame on their heads." Don't let evil conquer you, but conquer evil by doing good."

Every one of us has sinned and we are all in need of forgiveness. The sins that we have committed may be different, but in God's eyes, we are all sinners. We all need a Savior. The great news is that we don't have to feel guilty or carry any shame! All we have to do to be free of our sin is to confess it to God! We have been given a free pass! Because Jesus died for our sins, we have been given the key to freedom, joy, and an abundant life! Ask God to show you what you need to confess, and then do it.

First Timothy 1:19 (NLT) says, "Cling to your faith in Christ, and keep your conscience clear. For some people have deliberately violated their consciences; as a result, their faith has been shipwrecked." God has given us a conscience so that we can recognize our sin and confess it. Ignoring your conscience will eventually make you numb to its voice, and lead to the complete destruction of your faith in God. As Dr. Gary Chapman has said, "Nothing is more fundamental to mental health, let alone spiritual health, than living with an empty conscience."[2]

If you are questioning and doubting God, confess it. If you are angry with Him because you don't understand what is happening in your life, confess that. It is the first step you must take on the bridge to healing, restoration, and joy. Even in the midst of unspeakable pain, we must recognize God's sovereignty.

Author Diane Moody said, "If we truly believe He is who He says He is, then we must acknowledge His sovereignty and know within our heart of hearts that what He allows to happen to us always has a purpose. Even on the darkest night. Even when our souls cry out in unspeakable pain. Even when we can't face another day. Even when we can't sense His presence. We hold on because we know He's holding on to us as well—whether it feels like it or not."[3]

Dear friend, if you are hurting right now, you don't have to carry that pain any longer. You can experience forgiveness, freedom, and joy! Ask God to show you what you need to confess. He will be faithful to bring it to your mind, because He longs to have a restored relationship with you. He has never stopped loving you, and He is patiently waiting for you to admit your sin, so that He can set you free from it. Don't wait another moment for your freedom. You can experience it right now! If you're not sure what to say, just pray this prayer:

Dear Heavenly Father, Your Word says, that we will know the truth, and the truth will set us free (John 8:32). I want to know the truth and I want to be free. I admit that I am a sinner. I ask you to show me the sins in my life that I need to confess. I humble myself before you and surrender my life to you. I thank you for sending Jesus to cleanse me from all my sins, and I accept Him as my Savior. Amen.

After you have prayed, take a few moments to sit quietly and let God reveal to you specific times when you were disobedient to His Word. With every sin that comes to your mind, ask God to forgive you. Be specific about your sins. Say them out loud so that they are exposed to the light and lose their power over you.

Don't be surprised if you find yourself weeping as you acknowledge your sin. Oftentimes, when we realize how much we have hurt our Father, we experience grief. But don't worry. This is a healthy reaction! James 4:9 (NLT) says, "Let there be tears for the wrong things you have done. Let there be sorrow and deep grief."

The good news is that we don't have to stay sad! Remember 1 John 1:9 (NLT), "But if we confess our sins to him, he is faithful and just to forgive us our sins and to cleanse us from all wickedness." Receive His forgiveness and thank Him for it! We can rejoice with happy tears, because all of our sins have been washed away! Psalm 103:12 (NLT) tells us that God "has removed our sins as far from us as the east is from the west." When you confess, you are free, precious friend! Through confession, you are free.

Make it personal:

1. What did King Saul neglect to do when he was confronted with his sin?

2. What did King David do when he was confronted with his sin?

3. What is the first thing you should do when you realize you have sinned?

4. What is the first thing you should do when you don't love someone, or you don't want to be obedient to God?

5. Why does your confession affect your ability to experience joy?

6. Did the Holy Spirit show you anything that you need to confess? If so, I pray you will confess it to Jesus and experience forgiveness, freedom, and joy!

CHAPTER FOUR

A Better Way

Confession can be sweet. Doesn't it feel good to get something off your chest? After our disobedience has been exposed, we may feel a deep sense of relief. We may even feel a sense of happiness. The burden of keeping a sin hidden is a heavy one to carry and it can feel great to drop that load.

But before you get too comfortable with your newfound freedom, you can't stop there. In order to go all the way across the bridge, you have to keep going and take the next step. Confession is the first step to joy and freedom, but it's not the only one.

Read what God spoke to David's son Solomon, the reigning king of Israel, in 2 Chronicles 7:12–14 (NLT),

"One night the LORD appeared to Solomon and said, 'I have heard your prayer and have chosen this Temple as the place for making sacrifices. At times I might shut up the heavens so that no rain falls, or command grasshoppers to devour your crops, or send plagues among you. Then if my people who are called by my name will humble themselves and pray and seek my face and turn from their wicked ways, I will hear from heaven and will forgive their sins and restore their land.'"

When any type of trouble comes into our life, it is very tempting to be angry with God and to assume that we have been unjustly wronged. But God's ways are perfect, and He knows exactly what we need. He loves us and promises to bless us. Sometimes that means He will allow us to experience suffering, in order to change us and to draw us closer to Him. Blessings come in all shapes, sizes, and all types of packages.

When we humble ourselves, we admit we are sinners who need God and need a Savior. It is healing and refreshing to recognize our sin and to confess it. But we can't stop there. We must make a turn away from that sin and go in a new direction if we want the joy that Jesus promised us. We have to stop disobeying God and then turn toward God, or in other words, go in the direction He commands us to go. Once we confess our sin, our love for God should lead us to repentance, which means we stop committing that sin. Then, we need to choose to obey whatever God is telling us to do.

Throughout the Gospels, Jesus told the people, "Repent of your sins and turn to God." He taught His disciples to preach that as well. Webster's dictionary tells us the word repent means "to turn from sin and dedicate oneself to the amendment of one's life."

Read what the author wrote in the tenth chapter of the book of Hebrews, beginning with verse 26 through verse 39 (NLT):

"Dear friends, if we deliberately continue sinning after we have received knowledge of the truth, there is no longer any sacrifice that will cover these sins. There is only the terrible expectation of God's judgment and the raging fire that will consume his enemies. For anyone who refused to obey the law of Moses was put to death without mercy on the testimony of two or three witnesses. Just think how much worse the punishment will be for those who have trampled on the Son of God, and have treated the blood of the covenant, which made us holy, as if it were common and unholy, and have insulted and disdained the Holy Spirit who brings God's mercy to us. For we know the one who said, "I will take revenge. I will pay them back."

He also said, "The LORD will judge his own people."

It is a terrible thing to fall into the hands of the living God.

"Think back on those early days when you first learned about Christ. Remember how you remained faithful even though it meant terrible suffering. Sometimes you were exposed to public ridicule and were beaten, and sometimes you helped others who were suffering the same things. You suffered along with those who were thrown into jail, and when all you owned was taken from you, you accepted it with joy. You knew there were better things waiting for you that will last forever.

"So do not throw away this confident trust in the Lord. Remember the great reward it brings you! Patient endurance is what you need now, so that you will continue to do God's will. Then you will receive all that he has promised.

"For in just a little while, the Coming One will come and not delay. And my righteous ones will live by faith. But I will take no pleasure in anyone who turns away."

But we are not like those who turn away from God to their own destruction. We are the faithful ones, whose souls will be saved."

The Holy Spirit will be faithful to reveal our sin to us, but then we need to respond with repentance. If we don't choose to turn back to God, eventually we will become tormented with guilt and we'll feel worse than we ever did before. But if we turn back to God and turn away from our sin, we will experience indescribable joy and the great reward He has for us, both now and in eternity! We can choose joy!

In the eighth chapter of the book of John, Jesus taught the people about the forgiveness and mercy of God by showing forgiveness and mercy to a woman who was accused of adultery. Jesus did not condemn her, but He told her to "go and sin no more." Then He said to the people, "If you follow me, you won't have to walk in darkness, because you will have the light that leads to life."

Jesus did not condemn the woman, but He told her that she must stop sinning. He went on to say that following Him was the only way to experience life. Sin keeps us bound in darkness and despair. Repentance and obedience lead to an abundant life, full of the joy of the Lord.

Two Confessions, Two Different Directions

In the Gospels, we can read about two of Jesus's disciples who were confronted with their sins. They both confessed them, but only one man chose to repent and turn back to God. Their lives ended in two completely different ways.

Judas

Matthew 27:3–5 (NLT)

When Judas, who had betrayed him, realized that Jesus had been condemned to die, he was filled with remorse. So he took the thirty pieces of silver back to the leading priests and the elders. "I have sinned," he declared, "for I have betrayed an innocent man."

"What do we care?" they retorted. "That's your problem."

Then Judas threw the silver coins down in the Temple and went out and hanged himself.

Peter

Matthew 26:69–75 (NLT)

Meanwhile, Peter was sitting outside in the courtyard. A servant girl came over and said to him,

"You were one of those with Jesus the Galilean."

But Peter denied it in front of everyone. "I don't know what you're talking about," he said.

Later, out by the gate, another servant girl noticed him and said to those standing around, "This man was with Jesus of Nazareth."

Again Peter denied it, this time with an oath. "I don't even know the man," he said.

A little later some of the other bystanders came over to Peter and said, "You must be one of them; we can tell by your Galilean accent."

Peter swore, "A curse on me if I'm lying—I don't know the man!" And immediately the rooster crowed.

Suddenly, Jesus's words flashed through Peter's mind: "Before the rooster crows, you will deny three

times that you even know me." And
he went away, weeping bitterly.

John 21:1–7 (NLT)

Later, Jesus appeared again
to the disciples beside the Sea of
Galilee. This is how it happened.
Several of the disciples were there—
Simon Peter, Thomas (nicknamed
the Twin), Nathanael from Cana in
Galilee, the sons of Zebedee, and
two other disciples.
Simon Peter said, "I'm going fishing."

"We'll come, too," they all
said. So they went out in the boat,
but they caught nothing all night.

At dawn Jesus was standing
on the beach, but the disciples
couldn't see who he was. He called
out, "Fellows, have you caught any
fish?"

"No," they replied.

Then he said, "Throw out
your net on the right-hand side of

the boat, and you'll get some!" So they did, and they couldn't haul in the net because there were so many fish in it.

Then the disciple Jesus loved said to Peter, "It's the Lord!" When Simon Peter heard that it was the Lord, he put on his tunic (for he had stripped for work), jumped into the water, and headed to shore.

When Judas realized he had sinned, he admitted it. But he didn't turn back to God, ask for forgiveness, and change his ways. Instead, he let his guilt and shame drive him to madness and he took his own life. How tragic! Guilt and shame without repentance are powerful, and they can completely destroy our lives.

Peter's response to his own sin was very different. He wept bitterly when he realized that he had denied Jesus. He knew he had sinned, and he felt great remorse. But days later, when he discovered that Jesus was alive, he was so eager to be with him that he couldn't even wait for the boat to take him to the shore. He jumped into the water, and raced to the beach to be with Jesus!

Peter may have denied Jesus before and turned his back on God. But when Peter realized that it was Jesus who enabled them to catch all those fish, I think he understood that Jesus still loved him and had forgiven him. He didn't let his guilt, shame, or pride keep him from turning back to Jesus. I think he was overwhelmed with relief and immensely grateful that he had been forgiven. He had experienced life without Jesus, and he knew that it wasn't worth living. In his excitement, he just couldn't contain himself. He jumped in to the water and raced to the shore out of his intense love and appreciation for his Lord!

Step Two and Three: Repent and Obey

When we are confronted with our sin, we always have a choice. Like Peter, we can confess it and repent. We can turn back to God and experience a sweet reunion with Him. Or we can choose to live in darkness and sadness, separated from

God, like Judas did. God is always willing to forgive us and He longs for us to return to Him. But ultimately, it is our choice.

> "Now listen! Today I am giving you a choice between life and death, between prosperity and disaster. For I command you this day to love the LORD your God and to keep his commands, decrees, and regulations by walking in his ways. If you do this, you will live and multiply, and the LORD your God will bless you and the land you are about to enter and occupy.
>
> "But if your heart turns away and you refuse to listen, and if you are drawn away to serve and worship other gods, then I warn you now that you will certainly be destroyed. You will not live a long, good life in the land you are crossing the Jordan to occupy.

"Today I have given you the choice between life and death, between blessings and curses. Now I call on heaven and earth to witness the choice you make. Oh, that you would choose life, so that you and your descendants might live! You can make this choice by loving the LORD your God, obeying him, and committing yourself firmly to him. This is the key to your life. And if you love and obey the LORD, you will live long in the land the LORD swore to give your ancestors Abraham, Isaac, and Jacob." (Deuteronomy 30:15–20, NLT)

God spoke these words to the Israelites before they entered the Promised Land, and they are still relevant to us today. We can choose a life of blessing, by doing what God tells us to do, or we can choose a life of suffering, by ignoring God's Word and doing what we want to do.

Confession comes from our mouth, but first it takes place in our heart and mind. On the other hand, repentance and obedience require actions. The words repent and obey are verbs. We need to do something to *show* our repentance and obedience.

What sin did God reveal to you? What does "turning back to God" look like for you? Some sins have an obvious path to correction. For example, if you told a lie, you can confess it and then stop lying. If you cheated, confess it and stop cheating. If you've been unable or unwilling to forgive, confess it and then choose to forgive.

But don't forget James 4:17 (NLT), "Remember, it is sin to know what you ought to do and then not do it." Perhaps the Holy Spirit revealed something to you that you *should* have been doing. Maybe you have been ignoring the voice of God, telling you to change your diet, or to exercise regularly, or visit your neighbor, or donate to a charity. Maybe God has been speaking to you about volunteering at your church, or applying for a new job, but your fear has kept you from obeying Him.

Dear friend, don't let anything rob you of the joy and blessings God has for you when you obey Him. I have been there, and I have been miserable! There have been times in my life when my fear or anxiety or selfishness made me so slow to obey, that I never obeyed. I have realized that procrastination is just another road to disobedience. Trust me, you don't want to go down that road. It is a dead end.

Choose today to repent and obey whatever God is telling you to do. If you want to experience joy, then repentance and obedience must become a daily choice, a lifestyle. If God wants you to apologize to your spouse, do it. If you need to forgive someone, remember that God has forgiven you and choose to forgive. If God has been leading you to home school your kids, leave your job, move to a new city, talk to your co-worker about Jesus, start a business, write a book, or anything else, just do it. You will never, ever regret obedience, but you could spend the rest of your life regretting disobedience.

Jonah

One of my favorite examples of this truth is found in the book of Jonah. If you haven't read it, take a moment to do so. It is one of the shortest books in the Bible, but it's full of powerful lessons. I probably like the story of Jonah because I can relate to him in a lot of ways. I think I'm a little like Jonah. I can sympathize with him.

God told Jonah to do something, and Jonah didn't want to do it, so he tried to run away from the Lord. Now that is really funny to me because I know Scripture. I know that there isn't any place we can go to get away from the Lord. But even though I know God sees everything I do, and He knows my every thought, if I don't want to obey Him, I still try to hide! I may not get on a boat or go to another city, but I can be very good at ignoring God's voice and pretending He doesn't see my disobedience. That's so silly!

I think Jonah knew in his heart that He couldn't get away from God. But his fear of the people of Nineveh was so strong that it caused him to be irrational, so he tried. He got on a boat and went in the opposite direction. Then God exposed his disobedience by sending a violent storm, nearly capsizing the boat. Eventually, the sailors on the boat drew lots to see which one of them had offended the gods and caused the storm. The lot fell on Jonah. Jonah confessed that he had been running from God, but he still wasn't willing to obey God and go to Nineveh. He decided he would rather be dead or take his chances in the sea, so he told them to throw him overboard!

How often have we put ourselves into horrible situations, just like Jonah, simply because we don't want to obey God? I know I have been guilty of doing that. I have suffered the consequence of it too, and it has not been pleasant.

I believe we do that because we don't understand God's love for us. When we run from Him, it's because we don't trust Him. We are afraid that what He is asking us to do will be too difficult, uncomfortable, frightening, painful, or rob us of something that we really want. We are afraid that somehow it will make our lives less happy.

That, dear friend, couldn't be further from the truth. That is what our adversary, the devil, wants us to believe. He is always working hard to keep us from obeying God. He knows the truth. He knows that God loves us, wants to bless us, and wants to use us to further His Kingdom. The devil hates God and he hates you. He knows that the abundant, joyful life that Jesus promised you will only be experienced when you obey God, so he will do anything he can to stop you from doing that.

After Jonah was thrown into the sea, he sank deep into the ocean and became tangled in seaweed. He thought he was going to die, but God sent a giant fish to swallow him. He spent three days and nights inside the fish. I can't even imagine how awful it was to be inside a fish's belly! I'm sure it was utter darkness, probably painfully uncomfortable, smelly, slimy, and frightening. And to make matters worse, Jonah had no idea how or when the horrible torture would end.

Inside the fish, Jonah finally realized that the only way he would find peace was through obedience. He confessed, repented, and agreed to do what God had told him to do. He sang songs of praise to God, and then the fish spit him up on the beach.

If we want to experience joy, if we want the abundant life that Jesus came to give us, we have to do as Jonah did. We must humble ourselves by admitting that God is right and so, obviously we are wrong. We must confess, repent, and then do whatever God is asking us to do. If we don't fully obey Him, we will never move beyond our current circumstances. We will stay stuck "in the belly of the whale."

Jonah's story has an amazing ending. The people of Nineveh all turned to God! Jonah's obedience brought a huge revival! God still had to deal with Jonah's lack of love and compassion, and his ego, but nevertheless, Nineveh was saved!

Imagine what might happen if you obey and do what God is asking you to do. How many people might be saved for eternity? What might happen in your marriage, or your family? And the added bonus is you will experience joy and blessings! Complete obedience will always lead to an abundant life, full of joy.

Obedience can be hard, but living a life full of guilt, depression, anger, shame, anxiety, or fear is so much harder. Philippians 2:13 (NLT) tells us,

"God is working in you, giving you the desire to obey Him, and the power to do what pleases Him." God wants you to obey Him, but He also wants to help you obey Him. If you're having a hard time obeying God, ask Him to work in you and to give you the desire and the power to obey. He will do it!

It's important that we acknowledge that we can't live the way God wants us to live simply by using our own strength or determination. We need the power of the Holy Spirit. Whenever we admit that we are weak or unable, God can prove Himself to be strong and capable for us. He said, "My grace is all you need. My power works best in weakness" (2 Corinthians 12:9, NLT). Second Timothy 1:7 (NLT) tells us, "God has not given us a spirit of fear and timidity, but of power, love, and self-discipline." When we humble ourselves and ask God for His help, He fills us with His Spirit. God's Spirit gives us the power, love, and self-discipline we need to be able to obey Him.

God wants you to cross the bridge. He wants you to leave your old life behind and come over to the new life He has created for you. So take the steps, no matter how hard they may seem. Nothing is as painful or difficult as staying where you are. Confess, repent, obey, and experience joy.

Make it personal:

1. What does it mean to repent?

2. What did Judas do after he confessed his sin?

3. What did Peter do after he confessed his sin?

4. If you want to experience joy, what must you do after you confess your sin?

5. Have you discovered a lack of obedience in your life? Is there something God wants you to do that you haven't done?

If so, I pray you will confess it right now, repent, and choose to obey today.

6. How will your obedience affect your life?

CHAPTER FIVE

The Power in Our Words

If you have applied the principles that I have shared with you, then you have made it through the most difficult steps across the bridge! The rest of the journey is so much easier! But you haven't reached the other side yet so don't look back. Don't doubt what you've done or how far you have come. Just keep moving. You can easily be tempted to go back to where you came from if you don't take the next few steps.

In the last chapter, I explained that we need God's power in order to do what God wants us to do. We can't live the life God wants us to live on our own strength or determination. If we try to do that, we will fail. We won't experience the joy and peace that Jesus promised us. Instead, we will experience frustration, confusion, and doubt.

God chooses to display His power through His people, but He doesn't force His power on anyone. He invites us to partner with Him, but He has given us the choice. We can choose to plug into His power, live an amazing life, and do incredible things. Or we can choose to reject His power and struggle every day just to survive.

God doesn't want to control you. He wants a relationship with you based on mutual love. He wants you to obey Him so He can bless you and reveal more of His love to you. The more you trust and obey Him, the more you will see Him fulfill His promises to you and the more you will experience His love and His power. He will transform you and make you into a new person, with a new life!

One of the ways we can have direct access to God's power is simply through our words. I think this is fascinating! When we pray, our words connect us to His power. James 5:16 (NLT), "Confess your sins to each other and pray for each other so that you may be healed. The earnest prayer of a righteous person has great power and produces wonderful results." Our prayers have great power and they bring results!

God has given us the power to change our lives simply by using our words! However, we have been given the choice to do good, or to do harm with them. Proverbs 18:21 (NIV) says, "The tongue has the power of life and death, and those who love it will eat its fruit." The New Living Translation says it this way, "Those who love to talk will experience the consequences, for the tongue can kill or nourish life." Stop and think about that for a moment. Our words have the power to produce death or life! The Message Bible makes it even simpler to understand. "Words kill, words give life; they're either poison or fruit—you choose."

The book of Proverbs has a lot to say about our words.

> "The words of the wicked
> are like a murderous ambush, but
> the words of the godly save lives."
> (Proverbs 12:6, NLT)

"From the fruit of their lips people are filled with good things." (Proverbs 12:14a, NIV)

"From the fruit of their lips people enjoy good things." (Proverbs 13:2a, NIV)

"A fool's proud talk becomes a rod that beats him, but the words of the wise keep them safe." (Proverbs 14:3, NLT)

"Kind words are like honey—sweet to the soul and healthy for the body." (Proverbs 16:24, NLT)

"Wise words satisfy like a good meal; the right words bring satisfaction." (Proverbs 18:20, NLT)

James also warns us about the power of our words in chapter 3, beginning with verse 2 through verse 10 (NLT).

"Indeed, we all make many mistakes. For if we could control

our tongues, we would be perfect and could also control ourselves in every other way. We can make a large horse go wherever we want by means of a small bit in its mouth. And a small rudder makes a huge ship turn wherever the pilot chooses to go, even though the winds are strong. In the same way, the tongue is a small thing that makes grand speeches. But a tiny spark can set a great forest on fire. And among all the parts of the body, the tongue is a flame of fire. It is a whole world of wickedness, corrupting your entire body. It can set your whole life on fire, for it is set on fire by hell itself. People can tame all kinds of animals, birds, reptiles, and fish, but no one can tame the tongue. It is restless and evil, full of deadly poison. Sometimes it praises our Lord and Father, and sometimes it curses those who have been made in the image of God. And so blessing and cursing come pouring out of the same mouth. Surely, my brothers and sisters, this is not right!"

James describes the tongue as a flame that "can set your whole life on fire." Think about that for a moment. Fire can be a good thing or a bad thing. A fire can bring light, warmth, beauty, joy, a sweet aroma, precious memories, relaxation, and the enjoyable sounds of crackling and popping. It can be used for cooking food, making hot drinks, providing a signal, or a pleasant gathering place for fellowship or romance.

But as you know, fire can also cause incredible harm and damage very quickly. It can destroy acres of forests and homes within a few short hours. It can consume a lifetime of memorabilia in an instant and bring intense physical pain and death to every living creature.

The effects of fire are determined by the way it is used. Contained and managed correctly, fire brings joy and preserves life. Mismanaged or out of control, fire causes damage and death. So it is with our words.

The Power in Our Thoughts

Our words truly are powerful! When we use our words to grumble, complain, criticize, ridicule, or blame, we are speaking words of death to everyone who hears us, including ourselves. When we use our words to thank, praise, compliment, encourage, and inspire, we are speaking words of life to everyone who hears us, including ourselves. That is why we must choose to use our words to bring life and not death.

James tells us that no one can tame the tongue, so then, how is it possible to do so? How can we consistently speak words that bring life to ourselves and to others? The answer is simple. We think before we speak. This isn't a strategy. It is just a fact. Before you say anything, it is first a thought. Our thoughts control our words. So if we want to control our words, we must first control our thoughts.

THE POWER IN OUR WORDS

"For whatever is in your heart determines what you say." (Matthew 12:34, NLT)

In our culture, we refer to the *mind* as the place where we reason and think. But the Bible often refers to the *heart* as being the place where we think, as well as the place where we feel. It stands for man's entire mental and moral activity. So the words *heart* and *mind* can be interchangeable in Scripture. Matthew 9:4 and Psalm 19:14 are examples of this. According to Scripture, the things we think about come from our mind and our heart. In Luke 6:45 (NLT), Jesus said, "A good person produces good things from the treasury of a good heart, and an evil person produces evil things from the treasury of an evil heart. What you say flows from what is in your heart." In other words, what you say flows from what is in your mind.

> "Those who are dominated by the sinful nature think about sinful things, but those who are controlled by the Holy Spirit think about things that please the Spirit. So letting your sinful nature con-

> trol your mind leads to death.
> But letting the Spirit control your
> mind leads to life and peace. For
> the sinful nature is always hostile to
> God. It never did obey God's laws,
> and it never will. That's why those
> who are still under the control of
> their sinful nature can never please
> God." (Romans 8:5–8, NLT)

Whatever is in your mind controls what you say. Likewise, whatever you are saying will dramatically influence what you are thinking about. You can't sing the lyrics to one song while simultaneously thinking about another. You can't speak words of hope while thinking about suicide. Your brain and your mouth work together not separately.

Let's look at this passage from Philippians chapter 4:4–9 (NLT):

> "Always be full of joy in the
> Lord. I say it again—rejoice! Let
> everyone see that you are consid-

erate in all you do. Remember, the Lord is coming soon.

"Don't worry about anything; instead, pray about everything. Tell God what you need, and thank him for all he has done. Then you will experience God's peace, which exceeds anything we can understand. His peace will guard your hearts and minds as you live in Christ Jesus.

"And now, dear brothers and sisters, one final thing. Fix your thoughts on what is true, and honorable, and right, and pure, and lovely, and admirable. Think about things that are excellent and worthy of praise. Keep putting into practice all you learned and received from me—everything you heard from me and saw me doing. Then the God of peace will be with you."

How do we fix our thoughts on what is true, right, and worthy of praise? The Bible is our greatest source of truth, and it tells us what is right and worthy of praise. Whenever we are tempted to think unhealthy or unlovely thoughts, we need to redirect our thoughts to whatever is in God's Word.

Second Timothy 3:16, 17 (NLT) says, "All Scripture is inspired by God and is useful to teach us what is true and to make us realize what is wrong in our lives. It corrects us when we are wrong and teaches us to do what is right."

Colossians 3:2, 3 (NLT) instructs us to, "Think about the things of heaven, not the things of earth. For you died to this life, and your real life is hidden with Christ in God."

When we think the wrong things, we begin to feel the wrong things. What you think, you will feel. What you feel, you have been thinking. Think about what you have been thinking. That will explain why you feel the way you do. And when you think the wrong things, you say the wrong things and then you do the wrong things.

Fear, sadness, worry, anger, and every destructive emotion we have experienced first began in our mind. This is what has been referred to as stinkin' thinkin' and we need to get rid of it. Don't *believe* everything you think. The Bible tells us that Satan is the father of lies. He is constantly trying to get you to believe things that aren't true by planting lies in your mind. We need to replace those lies with the truth.

Second Corinthians 10:4, 5 (NIV) tells us, "The weapons we fight with are not the weapons of the world. On the contrary, they have divine power to demolish strongholds. We demolish arguments and every pretension that sets itself up against the knowledge of God, and we take captive every thought to make it obedient to Christ." The Bible says we have the ability to control our thoughts. We can think about whatever we choose to think about. Our thoughts do not have any power unless we give it to them.

The Message Bible says it like this, "The tools of our trade aren't for marketing or manipulation, but they are for demolishing that entire massively corrupt culture. We use our powerful God-tools for smashing warped philosophies, tearing down barriers erected against the truth of God, fitting every loose thought and emotion and impulse into the structure of life shaped by Christ."

We must become aware of the things we think about. Romans 12:2 (NLT) says, "Don't copy the behavior and customs of this world, but let God transform you into a new person by changing the way you think. Then you will learn to know God's will for you, which is good and pleasing and perfect." What we think, we say. What we say, we do, and what we do eventually determines who we become.

Margaret Thatcher was a British woman who had a big dream, a dream that started when she was just a girl. She became the longest-serving prime minister of the United Kingdom of the twentieth century, and the only woman ever to have held the post. Her father was a minister, as well as a politician, and he taught her the importance of her thoughts. I'm convinced that is the reason she was so strong and successful.

Margaret Thatcher has said that her father frequently told her, "Watch your thoughts, for they become words. Watch your words, for they become actions. Watch your actions, for they become habits. Watch your habits, for they become character. Watch your character, for it becomes your destiny."

Step Four: Speak Life

The fourth step you must take to get across the bridge to a new life and a new you is to speak positively. Speak words that bring life! Speak words full of thankfulness, and you will begin to feel joyful. Talk about God's promises to you, and you will begin to believe them and be filled with hope. Speak words of praise to God, and you will strengthen your faith in Him. Worship God, and your love for Him will grow.

After you have confessed your sins, humbled yourself before God, repented and made a decision to obey, confirm it with your words. Encourage yourself and recite the Bible verses that remind you that you are going in the right direction. Speak life, not words of defeat, destruction, discouragement, or death.

When you're struggling with negative emotions, don't constantly talk about how bad you feel.

Don't dwell on the things you wish you had or talk about what you're missing in your life. Instead, thank God for all the things that you do have. Speak words of thankfulness and praise to Him. Gratitude will immediately change your attitude. It is "the hallway" to that place of joy and peace that we all desire. The more you express your gratitude, the more thankful and joyful you will become. If you want to turn your depression into joy, then turn your anger and frustration into gratitude and praise.

If you have been putting yourself down, change the way you have been talking about yourself and start saying what God says about you. In Psalm 139, He says you are beautiful, wonderful, and His thoughts about you are precious! In Galatians 3:26, He calls you His child! Romans 8:35–39 says that nothing can ever separate you from God's love for you! Jesus said you are the light of the world, the salt of the earth, and a friend! The Bible has hundreds of verses that show us that God adores us and that He is pleased with us, His creation.

Revelation 12:10 (NLT) calls the devil "the accuser of the brothers and sisters." The devil works "day and night" to accuse you and to convince you that you are unlovable and worthless. He is a liar (John 8:44), and he will never stop trying to deceive you.

But for every negative word the devil speaks to you, God's Word has a rebuttal. God's Word is full of the truth, and we can use it to defeat every lie of the enemy. It is called our Sword of the Spirit in Ephesians 6. It is a weapon that will defeat the devil. This is why it is extremely valuable to memorize scriptures that encourage you and build up your faith. If you have a variety of Bible verses memorized, you can immediately "pull out your sword" when the devil attacks your thoughts and you can make him flee.

In Matthew chapter 4 and Luke chapter 4, Jesus used scripture to expose the lies of the devil and to resist every temptation. We can do the same. God's Word will always disarm the devil. The Bible is our greatest reliable source of powerful, life-giving words.

"For the word of God is alive and powerful. It is sharper than the sharpest two-edged sword, cutting between soul and spirit, between joint and marrow. It exposes our innermost thoughts and desires." (Hebrews 4:12, NLT)

"My child, pay attention to what I say. Listen carefully to my words. Don't lose sight of them. Let them penetrate deep into your heart, for they bring life to those who find them, and healing to their whole body. Guard your heart above all else, for it determines the course of your life. Avoid all perverse talk; stay away from corrupt speech." (Proverbs 4:20–24, NLT)

Romans 10:17 (NKJV) says, "So then faith comes by hearing, and hearing by the word of God." Hearing God's Word builds up your faith. If we want to experience joy, we need to fill our mind, our hearts, and our *mouths* consistently with God's Word. Speak life!

Make it personal:

1. What do your words have the power to produce?

2. How can you consistently speak life-giving words?

3. How do you control your thoughts?

4. How do we know what is true, right, and worthy of praise?

5. What is our greatest reliable source of powerful, life-giving words?

6. What will happen when you consistently speak words of life to yourself and to others?

CHAPTER SIX

The Power in Our Praise

We have come to the end of the bridge. You have one more step to take. You are almost ready to cross over into a new way of living, a life filled with joy. Confession has opened your eyes and cleared your conscience. Repentance and obedience have set you in the right direction, and God's Word has illuminated your path. Your uplifting words are creating life in your spirit and restoring your soul. Only the last step of the bridge is left, and it is the easiest step of all.

Step Five: Sing Praises

I don't know if I can adequately express the importance of this last step. Singing is an incredibly powerful and essential step to experiencing joy. It is also the easiest of all the steps because singing is fun!

There are countless benefits to singing. It makes us feel happier, but it is cheaper than medication or therapy, healthier than drinking, and in my opinion, more fun than exercise. Here are some of the numerous claims that have been made about the physical and emotional benefits of singing:

Physically

1. It exercises our lungs, tones up our muscles and diaphragm.
2. It can improve our sleep and decrease muscle tension.
3. It improves our aerobic capacity, benefitting our heart and circulation.
4. It tones our facial muscles.

5. It improves our posture.
6. It increases our mental concentration and memory.
7. It can help to open sinuses and respiratory tubes.
8. It releases pain-relieving endorphins.
9. It boosts our immune system, enabling us to fight disease.
10. It can be energizing.

Emotionally

1. It increases self-esteem.
2. It increases feelings of wellbeing.
3. It enhances mood.
4. It can reduce stress and anxiety.
5. It is spiritually uplifting.
6. It can increase confidence.
7. It encourages creativity.
8. It promotes bonding and emotional healing.
9. It evokes emotions.
10. It can reduce anger and depression.

Just to be clear, listening to music is not the same thing as singing. Listening to uplifting music can be helpful, but its power is not comparable to singing. Singing puts the uplifting words on our *lips*, as well as in our ears. As I explained earlier, it is *our words* that have the power of life and death. Singing uplifting words gives you the power to bring life to your soul.

Singing doesn't have to sound beautiful or perfect. I think the devil has convinced many Christians that they aren't able to sing, so they don't. But that is a lie! Satan understands the power of our worship, and he will do anything to keep us from praising God. He will try to convince us that we sound terrible, or that it doesn't really matter if we sing or not.

There are dozens of Bible verses that tell us to sing to the Lord, such as Psalms 9:11; 30:4; 33:1, 3; 47:6, 7; 68:4; 1 Cor. 14:15; Eph. 5:19; Col. 3:16; and James 5:13. God would never tell us to do something that we aren't able to do or that isn't important for us to do. The Psalms tell us to make a joyful noise to the Lord. See Psalms 66:1; 81:1; 95:1, 2; 98:4, 6; and 100:1. God doesn't care about your pitch or rhythm. He wants you to be obedient. He wants to hear your praise and worship.

When we worship God with songs of praise, we are acknowledging that He is our Lord. We are declaring His ways are best and that we trust Him. We are blessing Him with our words of love and adoration. We are thanking Him for all that He has done, and that pleases Him. Remember, He wants us to thank Him and praise Him at all times. Hebrews 13:15 (NLT) instructs us to "offer through Jesus a continual sacrifice of praise to God, proclaiming our allegiance to his name."

Psalm 100:2 (NLT) declares, "Come before him, singing with joy." Verse 4 says, "Enter His gates with thanksgiving; go into His courts with praise." Worshipping God brings us closer to Him, and in His presence we experience joy! (Psalm 16:11). When we thank God and praise Him, we turn our focus on to Him and off our problems. When we worship God, we drown out all the negative, toxic voices that try to discourage us. It's as if we are wearing a headset, and the only thing we can hear is the song we are singing.

Worshipping God brings blessings to our lives. In Exodus 23:25 (NIV), God said, "Worship the Lord your God, and His blessing will be on your food and water. I will take away sickness from you, and none will miscarry or be barren in your land. I will give you a full life span."

Nothing makes me happier than when my children thank me, praise me, or express their love for me. It melts my heart, and I will do almost anything for them when they do it. If you are a parent, you know exactly what I'm talking about. God is our loving Father. He loves to hear His children thank Him, praise Him, and express their love to Him. When they do, He works on their behalf.

Singing Praises Defeats the Enemy

Second Chronicles 20:1–30 recounts the incredible story of how God delivered His people from their many enemies, after they used a "secret weapon" against them.

Jehoshaphat was the king of the nation of Judah, when the armies of three surrounding nations decided to combine their forces and declare war on Jehoshaphat. A messenger came and told Jehoshaphat about their plans. He said that a huge army was already marching their way, and this army was armed and ready to go to war.

Jehoshaphat was terrified by this news! He begged the LORD to tell him what to do and he ordered everyone in Judah to begin fasting. The people from all the towns of Judah came to the temple in Jerusalem, in order to pray and ask the LORD for help.

Jehoshaphat stood before the men, women, babies, and children of Judah and Jerusalem, in front of the new courtyard at the Temple of the LORD. He prayed:

> "O LORD, God of our ancestors, you alone are the God who is in heaven. You are ruler of all the kingdoms of the earth. You are powerful and mighty; no one can stand against you! O our God, did you not drive out those who lived in this land when your people Israel

arrived? And did you not give this land forever to the descendants of your friend Abraham? Your people settled here and built this Temple to honor your name. They said, 'whenever we are faced with any calamity such as war, plague, or famine, we can come to stand in your presence before this Temple where your name is honored. We can cry out to you to save us, and you will hear us and rescue us.'

"And now see what the armies of Ammon, Moab, and Mount Seir are doing. You would not let our ancestors invade those nations when Israel left Egypt, so they went around them and did not destroy them. Now see how they reward us! For they have come to throw us out of your land, which you gave us as an inheritance. O our God, won't you stop them? We are powerless against this mighty army that is about to attack us. We do not know what to do, but we are looking to you for help."

Then the Spirit of the LORD came upon one of the men standing there. His name was Jahaziel. He told them that God said, "Do not be afraid or discouraged by this mighty army, for the battle is not yours, but God's. You will not even need to fight. Take your positions; then stand still and watch the LORD's victory. He is with you, O people of Judah and Jerusalem. Do not be afraid or discouraged. Go out against them tomorrow, for the LORD is with you!"

After Jahaziel prophesied, King Jehoshaphat bowed down low with his face to the ground, worshiping the LORD. All the people of Judah and Jerusalem did the same.

Early the next morning, the army of Judah went out into the wilderness of Tekoa. On the way, Jehoshaphat stopped and said, "Listen to me, all you people of Judah and Jerusalem! Believe in the LORD your God, and you will be able to stand firm. Believe in his prophets, and you will succeed."

Then the king appointed singers to walk ahead of the army, singing to the LORD and praising him. They sang:

> "Give thanks to the LORD; his
> faithful love endures forever!"

At the very moment, they began to sing and give praise, the LORD caused the armies of Ammon, Moab, and Mount Seir to start attacking each other! So when the army of Judah arrived at the lookout point in the wilderness, all they saw were dead bodies lying on the ground as far as they could see! Not a single one of their enemies had escaped!

When King Jehoshaphat and his men realized what had happened, they decided to go out and gather up all the plunder. They found vast amounts of equipment, clothing, and other valuables—more than they could carry. There was so much plunder that it took them three days just to collect it all!

On the fourth day, they took time to praise and thank the Lord for giving them victory over their enemies. Then all the men returned to Jerusalem, with Jehoshaphat leading the way. They were overjoyed! They marched into Jerusalem, loudly singing and playing their musical instruments in celebration. They marched right up to the Temple of the Lord.

When all the surrounding kingdoms heard that the Lord himself had fought against the enemies of Israel, the fear of God came over them. So Jehoshaphat's kingdom was at peace from then on and God gave him rest.

I think that story is amazing! It's a beautiful illustration of God's desire and ability to defeat our enemies for us when we choose to sing praise and thanks to the Lord. When we are in a spiritual battle, worship has the power to defeat our enemy, the devil. Worship is our weapon!

Jonah experienced the power of worship when he was inside the whale. Jonah prayed to God saying, "But I will offer sacrifices to you with songs of praise, and I will fulfill all my vows. For my salvation comes from the Lord alone." Then the Lord ordered the fish to spit Jonah out onto the beach (Jonah 2:9–10, NLT). Jonah's trouble ended as soon as he surrendered to God's will and sang songs of praise.

The apostle Paul also used this powerful weapon. In Acts 16:22–40 (NLT), read what happened to Paul and Silas when they sang hymns to God:

"A mob quickly formed against Paul and Silas, and the city officials ordered them stripped and beaten with wooden rods. They were severely beaten, and then they were thrown into prison. The jailer was ordered to make sure they didn't escape. So the jailer put them into the inner dungeon and clamped their feet in the stocks.

"Around midnight Paul and Silas were praying and singing hymns to God, and the other prisoners were listening. Suddenly, there was a massive earthquake, and the prison was shaken to its foundations. All the doors immediately flew open, and the chains of every prisoner fell off! The jailer woke up to see the prison doors wide open. He assumed the prisoners had escaped, so he drew his sword to kill himself. But Paul shouted to him, 'Stop! Don't kill yourself! We are all here!'

"The jailer called for lights and ran to the dungeon and fell down trembling before Paul and Silas. Then he brought them out and asked, "Sirs, what must I do to be saved?"

"They replied, 'Believe in the Lord Jesus and you will be saved, along with everyone in your household.' And they shared the word of the Lord with him and with all who lived in his household. Even at that hour of the night, the jailer cared for them and washed their wounds. Then he and everyone in his household were immediately baptized. He brought them into his house and set a meal before them, and he and his entire household rejoiced because they all believed in God.

"The next morning the city officials sent the police to tell the jailer, 'Let those men go!' So the jailer told Paul, 'The city officials have said you and Silas are free to leave. Go in peace.'

"But Paul replied, 'They have publicly beaten us without a trial and put us in prison—and we are Roman citizens. So now they want us to leave secretly? Certainly not! Let them come themselves to release us!'

"When the police reported this, the city officials were alarmed to learn that Paul and Silas were Roman citizens. So they came to the jail and apologized to them. Then they brought them out and begged them to leave the city. When Paul and Silas left the prison, they returned to the home of Lydia.

There they met with the believers
and encouraged them once more.
Then they left town."

Paul and Silas were set free from prison when
they sang songs of praise to God. God gave them
their freedom and great favor with the jailer. They
were able to lead him and his family to the Lord.
They even received an apology from the city officials! God works on our behalf when we praise
Him.

Complaining Destroys Our Blessings

I think it's also important to learn from the
biblical accounts of people who chose *not* to worship or give thanks to God during their difficult
circumstances. For example, after God set the
Israelites free from slavery in Egypt, they had a
terrible habit of complaining about their lead-
ers and their circumstances. You can read about
their journey through the wilderness in the book
of Numbers. In Numbers 14:26–38 (NLT), you

can see how the Lord responded to their constant whining and complaining:

> "Then the LORD said to Moses and Aaron, "How long must I put up with this wicked community and its complaints about me? Yes, I have heard the complaints the Israelites are making against me. Now tell them this: 'As surely as I live, declares the LORD, I will do to you the very things I heard you say. You will all drop dead in this wilderness! Because you complained against me, every one of you who is twenty years old or older and was included in the registration will die. You will not enter and occupy the land I swore to give you. The only exceptions will be Caleb son of Jephunneh and Joshua son of Nun.
>
> "'You said your children would be carried off as plunder.

Well, I will bring them safely into the land, and they will enjoy what you have despised. But as for you, you will drop dead in this wilderness. And your children will be like shepherds, wandering in the wilderness for forty years. In this way, they will pay for your faithlessness, until the last of you lies dead in the wilderness.

"'Because your men explored the land for forty days, you must wander in the wilderness for forty years—a year for each day, suffering the consequences of your sins. Then you will discover what it is like to have me for an enemy.' I, the LORD, have spoken! I will certainly do these things to every member of the community who has conspired against me. They will be destroyed here in this wilderness, and here they will die!"

"The ten men Moses had sent to explore the land—the ones who incited rebellion against the LORD with their bad report—were struck dead with a plague before the LORD. Of the twelve who had explored the land, only Joshua and Caleb remained alive."

Whoa! Not one of the complainers was allowed to enter the land that was promised to them. Instead, they lived out the rest of their lives in the wilderness. That was not what God wanted. He wanted to give them a life of abundance in a land overflowing with blessings. But they never received His gift because their mouths were full of complaining rather than praise and thanksgiving.

Everyone who was twenty years old or older eventually died in the wilderness. Out of that entire generation of complainers, Joshua and Caleb were the only ones God allowed into The Promised Land. Those two men didn't complain about God or about their circumstances. On the contrary, they tried to encourage the people by praising the

Lord and reminding them of His power and His faithfulness.

> "They said to all the people of Israel, 'The land we traveled through and explored is a wonderful land! And if the LORD is pleased with us, he will bring us safely into that land and give it to us. It is a rich land flowing with milk and honey. Do not rebel against the LORD, and don't be afraid of the people of the land. They are only helpless prey to us! They have no protection, but the LORD is with us! Don't be afraid of them!' But the whole community began to talk about stoning Joshua and Caleb." (Numbers 14:7–10, NLT)

I wonder how often we spend needless time in "the wilderness" because of our complaining or our lack of praise and thanksgiving. Perhaps God has a blessing that He longs to give us, but He is waiting until we learn to give Him thanks and to praise Him in all circumstances. If we won't praise Him in the wilderness, maybe He knows we won't praise Him in The Promised Land either.

Worshipping God is a weapon that will defeat our enemy. It is also an act of gratitude, love, obedience, and the means by which we receive all of the blessings God has for us. Time spent in worship is never wasted. On the other hand, complaining doesn't accomplish anything for our good. In fact, when we complain, we are letting the devil use us to discredit God. When we complain about our situation, we are saying exactly what the devil wants us to say and damaging our lives with our own words.

Job Encounters God

The book of Job tells the story of another man who went through incredible pain and suffering. In the beginning of the story, Job handles his grief and pain with amazing integrity and godliness, even after his wife ridicules him.

"His wife said to him, 'Are you still trying to maintain your integrity? Curse God and die.' But Job replied, 'You talk like a foolish woman. Should we accept only good things from the hand of God and never anything bad?' So in all this, Job said nothing wrong." (Job 2:9–10, NLT)

But just seven days later, Job began to speak, and he let out a torrent of destructive words, cursing the day he was born, longing for death, and questioning God. He admitted that what happened to him was something he had always feared, he complained about his difficulties, and he declared that more trouble was coming.

"Oh, why give light to those in misery, and life to those who are bitter? They long for death, and it won't come. They search for death more eagerly than for hidden treasure. They're filled with joy when they finally die, and rejoice when they find the grave. Why is life given to those with no future, those God has surrounded with difficulties? I cannot eat for sighing; my groans pour out like water. What I always feared has happened to me. What I dreaded has come true. I have no peace, no quietness. I have no rest; only trouble comes." (Job 3:20–26, NLT)

I have a lot of compassion for Job. After all, he lost everything! I can't even imagine how devastating that would be and I can completely understand why he would have spoken the way he did. He was only human.

Throughout the rest of the book of Job, he continued to complain about his circumstances and he defended himself to his friends. He was not willing to accept any responsibility for his pain.

I don't judge him for doing that. I probably would have responded the same way under those conditions. He didn't have the Bible that we have now and he didn't know Jesus. He didn't know about Satan and how to defeat him. He did the best he could with what he had and with what he knew.

But then, God spoke to Job, and everything changed. In chapters 38 and 39, God reminded Job of His power, and He put Job in his place. In Job 40:3–5, Job admitted he had been wrong to question God and to complain. God continued to remind Job of His wisdom, justice, and might until Job finally repented and gave God the praise He deserves.

Job had an encounter with God that changed him forever. He understood that his complaining was sin, and for the first time in his life, he actually saw God. Job told God, "I know that you can do anything... I had heard about you before, but now I have seen you with my own eyes. I take back everything I said, and I sit in dust and ashes to show my repentance" (Job 42:2–6, NLT).

Job's suffering wasn't a punishment for his sin. Job 1:1 (NLT) tells us he "was blameless—a man of complete integrity." But Job let his suffering lead him into sin. He was angry about his pain, became prideful, and questioned God's wisdom, power and justice.

Job suffered miserably while he was questioning, complaining, and bitter. But when he had a change of heart, repented, and worshipped God, everything turned around for Job. Job forgave his friends, prayed for them, and their relationships were healed. Because Job praised God, God restored all his fortunes. In fact, God gave Job twice as much as he had before. He blessed Job in the second half of his life even more than in the beginning.

Worship Changes Us

The Lord longs for us to worship Him because He knows that *we* need it. Worship nourishes us and brings us blessings. When we worship God, our souls are refreshed and our minds are renewed. When Jesus said that He would give us "living water," He was referring to His Spirit. When we worship Jesus, we invite His Spirit into our lives. We need His Spirit inside of us, in order to be healed and whole. Unfortunately, sometimes we have to go through a period of drought or darkness to make us realize how much we need Him.

There was a drought in California for several years. The effects of the drought were noticeable everywhere, but I don't think anyone was as devastated by it as the farmers in the Central Valley. California farmers in the Central Valley grow an array of delicious fruits that require massive amounts of water. The summers in the Central Valley are usually hot and dry, so the farmers hope for plenty of winter rain to soak the ground around the fruit trees and fill up the groundwater reserves. Light summertime sprinkles alone can't produce sweet, juicy fruit. When there is an absence of winter rain, the trees suffer and produce a smaller, lesser quality fruit.

Other types of trees suffer from years of drought as well. Drought causes the leaves of a tree to fall off prematurely and dormancy sets in early. Even the enormous redwoods lose their strength as their roots become dry and brittle. Many of them fall over easily during a mild windstorm because the ground around them is also dry. Trees need heavy rain during the darkness and cold of winter, so the ground can absorb the moisture and the water can go all the way down to the roots, ensuring the tree will be able to stand during storms.

Psalm 1 says that people can be like trees that are planted along the riverbank, that bear fruit each season without fail and have leaves that never wither. Everything they do can prosper, under one condition. They must delight in doing everything the Lord wants.

When you choose to worship during times of hardship and darkness, during the winter of your soul, your spirit experiences the deep watering it is thirsting for. Our worship brings the rain we so desperately need to produce high quality fruit in our character.

The Lord is near to the brokenhearted and He heals them (Psalm 34:18, 147:3). His presence is with us when we are hurting. As we spend ample time with Him in the darkness, soaking up His spirit, we are transformed. Like a caterpillar in a cocoon, we change and turn into a beautiful butterfly.

THE POWER IN OUR PRAISE

As we worship God, we become more like Jesus. We become better, not bitter. We can accomplish more for His Kingdom. Our fruit will be sweeter and larger. Our roots will grow deep and become strong and able to keep us standing during every storm that life brings our way. We never have to be dormant and our leaves never have to wither. Worshipping God is good for us, and it's good for all our descendants. Look at Jeremiah 32:38–42 (NLT).

> "They will be my people, and I will be their God. And I will give them one heart and one purpose: to worship me forever, for their own good and for the good of all their descendants. And I will make an everlasting covenant with them: I will never stop doing good for them. I will put a desire in their hearts to worship me, and they will never leave me. I will find joy doing good for them and will faithfully and wholeheartedly replant them

in this land. 'This is what the LORD says: Just as I have brought all these calamities on them, so I will do all the good I have promised them.'" (Jeremiah 32:38–42)

Worship Is Always Rewarded

Psalm 69:30–31 (NLT) says, "I will praise God's name with singing, and I will honor him with thanksgiving. For this will please the LORD more than sacrificing cattle, more than presenting a bull with its horns and hooves." Nothing pleases God more than our praise. He wants everyone to praise Him, even children and infants. Psalm 8:2 (NLT) tells us, "You have taught children and infants to give you praise, silencing your enemies and all who oppose you." Jesus said if the people didn't praise Him, then the rocks would do it! (Luke 19:40) God wants to be praised!

When we worship God, we please Him, and when we please Him, He rewards us. Job, Jonah, Joshua and Caleb, Paul and Silas, Jehoshaphat, and many other biblical heroes received a reward after they praised the Lord. I believe that God will always reward us as well. Sometimes our worship will bring an immediate breakthrough in our situation, or an obvious answer to our prayers. Other times, we may not notice a change in our circumstances right away, but worshipping God will always make the devil flee and bring us into God's presence. One thing is for sure, when we worship Him with all our heart and mind and soul, we will experience joy, and there is no greater reward on earth.

Who Wants to Be Happy?

One of my favorite songs is the song "Happy" by Pharrell Williams. Apparently, a lot of other people enjoy this song as well. Here's what Wikipedia says about the song:

From Wikipedia, the free encyclopedia:

"Happy" is a midtempo soul and neo soul song on which

Williams's falsetto voice has been compared to Curtis Mayfield by critics. The song has been highly successful, peaking at No. 1 in the United States, United Kingdom, Canada, Ireland, New Zealand, and 19 other countries. It was the best-selling song of 2014 in the United States with 6.45 million copies sold for the year, as well as in the United Kingdom with 1.5 million copies sold for the year. It reached No. 1 in the UK on a record-setting three separate occasions and became the most downloaded song of all time in the UK in September 2014. It was nominated for an Academy Award for Best Original Song. A live rendition of the song won the Grammy Award for Best Pop Solo Performance at the 57th Annual Grammy Awards.

The music video for "Happy" was nominated for Best Male

Video and Video of the Year at the 2014 MTV Video Music Awards. It also won the Grammy Award for Best Music Video at the 57th Annual Grammy Awards. The song was *Billboard*'s number-one single for 2014. "Happy" was the most successful song of 2014, with 13.9 million units (sales plus equivalent streams) worldwide.

Wow, that's pretty impressive! Why do you think this particular song has done so well? I think it's because the song genuinely makes people feel happy! Try listening to it and staying in a bad mood. It's nearly impossible! People enjoy the song because they enjoy feeling happy.

Singing a happy song makes people feel happy, and the truth is, everyone really wants to feel happy. But happiness is a feeling that is temporary. On the other hand, the joy that comes from being in God's presence is a joy that will last forever. It doesn't depend on our circumstances. It comes from knowing the truth about who God is, what

He has done for us, how much He loves us, and who we are because of Him. It comes from knowing that we have nothing to fear, because we know He will always work on our behalf and do what is best for us. We can enjoy *everything* in life, when we trust God completely and stay in His presence.

We can feel God's presence with us no matter where we are and no matter what is happening in our lives. All we need to do is sing praises to Him. Singing to God will invite His Spirit into your life and will fill you with joy. Nothing that this life has to offer will ever compare to the joy that we can have in the presence of the Lord. Take the last step on the bridge. Leave your miserable life behind and cross over to the abundant, joyful life that God has for you. Make a joyful noise and sing to the Lord!

Make it personal:

1. What are some of the benefits of singing?

2. Why is singing more beneficial than listening to music?

3. Why should you worship God with songs of praise?

4. What will happen when you worship God with songs of praise during your difficult circumstances?

5. What will happen when you grumble and complain during your difficult circumstances?

6. If you have been complaining instead of thanking God, what should you do?

CHAPTER SEVEN

Transformed at the Cross

As I stated at the beginning of this book, I'm not content when there is a problem that I know can be fixed. I have to come up with a strategy to fix it. I wasn't able to figure out how to stay joyful, and that was a problem for me. I needed a solution, a process that would enable me to do that. I knew it was possible, because God doesn't tell us to do things without enabling us to do them. So I asked God to show me a way that would work for me, and He did.

One of the things I heard God say to me was, "Go to the cross." That didn't make sense to me at first. I had heard that phrase used many times before, and it always confused me. Was I supposed to pray at the cross? Was I supposed to confess my sins? Was I supposed to suffer like Christ at the cross? What exactly did that mean?

As I spent more time meditating on those words, and listening to the Holy Spirit, this acrostic came into my mind, and I believe it was inspired by the Holy Spirit.

C	Confess
R	Repent
O	Obey
S	Speak life
S	Sing praises

All of a sudden, the word "cross" had multiple meanings to me. I understood that "going to the cross" would serve as a reminder to me of all that Christ had done for me. It was a call to completely surrender my life to God, just as Christ had done. But the word CROSS was also an acronym for the process I could use to "cross over" to the place God wanted to take me.

In order for me to live a life of joy, meaning, and fulfillment, I needed to lay my life down at the cross, just like Jesus did. The way for me to do that was to first confess, repent, and obey. Then I needed to speak words of life to build my faith, and lastly, sing praises to God, in order to complete the process of surrender.

I had known in my head that surrendering to Jesus was something I was supposed to do, but for some reason, I just hadn't been able to do it consistently. Something always seemed to stand in the way. I think I assumed surrender meant more pain, so I avoided it. I had no idea that indescribable joy was on the other side of surrender.

The only thing I knew of surrender, was the surrender I had seen taking place in movies. In the movies I had seen, when someone was forced to surrender to their enemy after a battle, they had to give up their freedom. They were taken as prisoners, and usually treated very poorly. That was how I imagined it would be to surrender to God. For some reason, I feared He would take away all of my freedom and I would be treated like His slave.

But through my times of suffering, I discovered that surrendering to God was exactly the opposite of surrendering to an enemy. Surrendering to God gave me a much better life! As I surrendered, I realized that He was actually setting me free from the enemy who wanted to keep me imprisoned for the rest of my life.

God showed me that the cross was the way to a life of freedom and blessings. He wanted to rescue me from a life of bondage to sadness and despair. He didn't want to take me as His prisoner. He wanted to set me free!

When I finally understood this, I replayed a scene from another movie in my mind. In this movie, American soldiers arrived at the concentration camp in Auschwitz at the end of World War II. The Nazis had left, and the Americans came to tell the prisoners that the war was over and they were free. The prisoners were fearful at first, shocked and skeptical. They stayed inside their barracks and hid from the soldiers. But when they finally realized what was happening, they came out and accepted their freedom. They joyfully left the camp with the soldiers and went on to start a new life.

This is a much clearer illustration of what it means to surrender to God. He has come to rescue us from a life of misery and suffering. We can be afraid of Him, and remain in our own personal prison forever. Or we can trust Him, and allow Him to take us to a beautiful new life.

Once I understood that surrendering my life to God was the way to experiencing a better life, the Holy Spirit gave me the CROSS acronym. This gave me a step-by-step process to use, one that was easy for me to understand and remember. I finally understood the steps I needed to take to surrender and get back to where God wanted me to be. I discovered that by following this process I could get myself back on the right road, the road that leads to a life of joy and blessing.

The Bridge

One day, as I continued to meditate on this acronym, I saw a wooden bridge in my mind. The bridge was covered in fog, but as I got closer, I could see the first wooden plank. The word "CONFESS" was written on it. I stepped on to that plank, and I could see the second plank. The word "REPENT" was written on it. I took another step onto the next plank, and I saw that it contained the word "OBEY." I could see that there were only two more planks to cross on this bridge to get me to the other side of it. One plank had the words "SPEAK LIFE" written on it, and the next one contained the words "SING PRAISES." I stepped on each plank as I crossed this bridge, somehow knowing that it was very important not to skip over any of them.

As I finished my journey on the bridge and stepped off to the ground on the other side, the fog lifted. I was in a tropical paradise; more brilliant and glorious than any garden or park I have ever seen on earth. Everything about it was perfect for me. The temperature, the fragrances, and all the sights and sounds were my favorites. I was completely filled with joy and peace! Then I heard the voice of God say to me, "Welcome my daughter. All of this is for you. I hope you will stay here with Me forever."

THE BRIDGE

The air there was moist but not heavy. It was cool and clean. Jasmine, gardenias, roses, honeysuckles, lilacs, and numerous blossoming fruit trees lined my path and the fragrances were intoxicating. The sky was a cobalt blue, dotted with fluffy arctic white clouds. The perfectly manicured grass beneath my feet was soft and cold and I ran, jumped, and danced all over it without a bit of pain. I laughed, sang, and skipped around my paradise, stopping occasionally to pick a gorgeous bouquet of flowers or to enjoy a delicious piece of fruit.

I stopped for a moment to rest under a shady willow tree and I looked across the bridge. I saw the other side, the place I had left behind. I saw a man in a suit yelling at a woman working at a desk. The woman was crying. I saw another woman in a kitchen. She screamed and ran as a pan on the stove burst into flames. The flames quickly crawled up the wall, and engulfed the entire kitchen.

I saw a crying baby, standing up in a crib, alone in a dark room. I saw an elderly man slumped over in a wheelchair, a tear running down his cheek. I saw a young man covered with tattoos, smoking a cigarette, and drinking from a bottle. I saw a young pregnant woman, holding a razor in her hands and sobbing. I saw an older man cussing and banging on a slot machine. I saw a woman in a bathroom, wearing a glamorous gown and high heels, staring at a jar of pills.

I wanted to look away, but I couldn't. Sadness and anxiety came over me and I started to feel guilty for enjoying my paradise while there was so much pain and suffering going on just across the bridge. Then the fog rolled back in and the sky grew dark. A long, gray arm of fog wrapped itself around my waist and pulled me toward the bridge! I stepped onto the bridge and immediately I saw the words "SING PRAISES." I began to sing one of my favorite worship songs, and the arm released me.

I kept singing, and the fog began to lift. I kept singing and my paradise came back into view. I kept singing and the guilt, the sadness, and the anxiety all dissipated. Joy and peace returned to me and I was filled with an overwhelming sense of God's love for me.

The love I felt coming from God was so strong and so powerful I couldn't hold back my tears. His love filled me to a point of overflowing. I felt as if I would burst if I didn't give some of it away.

I looked across the bridge again, but this time I heard God say, "When you spend time with Me, you get to know Me. When you get to know Me, you can experience My love for you. When you experience My love for you, it is easy for you to love others. When you love others, you will be filled with joy. Don't let the sorrow of your world pull you back across the bridge. Stay in My presence. Love people, but stay in My presence and your life will always be joyful. When you are joyful, you bring light and hope into this dark and painful world. When you are joyful, people will be drawn to you. Then you can introduce them to Me, and they will be able to find salvation, joy, and an abundant life too. Guard your love and your joy! They are the best instruments you have to save the world."

The Lord knows me. He knows I'm a visual learner. I know He gave the vision of the bridge to me so that I would always remember *why* I need to "go to the cross." If I want to experience joy always, I must CROSS over the bridge, as often as necessary. There is a place full of love and joy waiting for me on the other side. It's waiting for you too. If we want to change the world, we must first be willing to let God change us.

Nothing to Lose, Everything to Gain!

Have you heard of the song called "Magic Penny" by Malvina Reynolds? Here are the lyrics:

Magic Penny
Love is something if you give it away,
Give it away, give it away.
Love is something if you give it away,
You end up having more.

It's just like a magic penny,
Hold it tight and you won't have any.
Lend it, spend it, and you'll have so many
They'll roll all over the floor.

For love is something if you give it away,
Give it away, give it away.
Love is something if you give it away,
You end up having more.

Money's dandy and we like to use it,
But love is better if you don't refuse it.
It's a treasure and you'll never lose it
Unless you lock up your door.

For love is something if you give it away,
Give it away, give it away.
Love is something if you give it away,
You end up having more.

This is a cute and simple song, but the concept is biblical. The Bible tells us that we will reap what we sow, and that whatever we give will come back to us, pressed down, shaken together and running over (Gal. 6:7, Luke 6:38). Jesus was the perfect example for us to follow. He gave His life for all of us out of His love for us, and then He received an eternal reward from the Father.

There is another acrostic that has helped me in my quest for joy. The word "joy" can be defined this way:

J	Jesus First
O	Others Second
Y	Yourself Last

When you put your relationship with Jesus first, everything else will fall into place. The more you express your love for Him, the more you will feel His love for you, and the more it overflows to others. The more you love others, the more you will receive from others. The more love you receive from others, the better you feel about yourself. You will begin to love yourself more too. So you really have nothing to lose, and everything to gain!

If you need joy, practice love. If you can't find the strength or desire to love, then go to the cross and CROSS over the bridge. Confess, repent, obey, speak life, and sing praises. If you've crossed the bridge and somehow you've lost your love and joy, you have probably slipped back over to the other side, so you need to CROSS over it again.

You Can Be Joyful Always!

I began writing this book to try to help people like me, who have battled with depression all of their lives, or struggled to experience joy on a daily basis. But after I began writing, I found myself desperately needing to follow my own advice, over and over again.

First, during the last few years, my heart was broken repeatedly, and I battled the discouragement that comes from feeling rejected, betrayed, and mistreated. As our foster-adopted children became teenagers, each one of them went through a difficult stage, as teenagers often do. They acted out in hurtful ways. I believed their wounds from their early childhood may have contributed to their behavior, but that didn't ease my pain. One by one, they seemingly turned against my husband and me and against everything we had taught them. As they became of age, each one of them left our home and brought tremendous heartache and stress into all of our lives.

Those years of family struggles could have been completely devastating, except for the miraculous power of God. In the midst of all we went through during that trying season, I had joy! The Lord has shown me how to genuinely experience joy in *every* situation. I have been thoroughly tried and tested. God has brought healing to our hearts, and our relationships have been restored. However, there was more to endure during that time of testing. While in the middle of those heartbreaking situations, I had to face some other challenges that made it much more difficult to keep my joy.

For nearly two years, I had been battling chronic pain from Achilles tendinitis. I was unable to walk or stand without experiencing sharp, intense pain. To make matters worse, I took a bad fall in the bathroom and smacked my ribs against the bathtub. For several weeks I was unable to breathe or move without pain. By the time my ribs were almost healed, I injured my collarbone, making it horribly painful to move again. The pain made it extremely difficult to exercise any part of my body, but the lack of movement only created more aches and pains.

During all this, my body was also recovering from adrenal fatigue and adjusting to a drastic, medically induced change in my hormone levels which caused sleep deprivation, continuous severe hot flashes, mood swings, and anxiety. Pain tends to make me irritable and highly emotional. How can God expect anyone to "rejoice always" when they are in constant pain and discomfort?

I also had to deal with the increasing absence of some of my closest friends. As my health problems persisted, I wasn't able to participate in the usual events and activities that we used to enjoy together. During this time, the Lord also called my husband and I to leave our church of thirty-plus years and commit to a newer church plant, so I stopped seeing many of them on a weekly basis, making it more difficult to stay in touch. I have been grieving the loss of all these relationships, and yet the Lord wants me to "consider it all joy"?

Lastly, as I write this book, I'm unemployed and my husband's employment is only seasonal.

Our income has been drastically reduced, and it is a challenge to pay for our monthly expenses.

A few years ago, the Lord made it very clear to me that my time in full-time pastoral ministry was over. At that time, I had total peace about leaving my employment, because my husband had a good job with benefits. I knew that leaving my ministry position would give me more time to write and to pursue other ministry opportunities.

But only one year later, Mark was told that his position had been eliminated and he was let go. That same day, right before he received that information, he had to respond to a call from a police officer, concerning an issue with a family member. That was a difficult and discouraging day, to say the least! God's Word says we should give thanks in all circumstances, but how are we supposed to be thankful for that?

Since then, Mark has only been able to find seasonal work, and I have not been able to find any work at all, mostly due to my health issues. One of our life-long dreams has been to take a road trip across the U.S. We had everything planned and booked, but when Mark lost his job, we had to postpone it. I was so disappointed! Am I still supposed to be thankful?

How can I possibly have joy, with all of these things happening in my life? Is that even possible? Yes, it is! I shared all that with you to encourage you to CROSS over the bridge. Just try it. It always works for me! While I'm in the middle of writing a book that explains the steps to experiencing the joy of the Lord all the time, I have had to practice these steps nearly every day. God has been faithful every day, and the joy of the Lord has always been available to me!

It's Going to Be Worth It!

It hasn't always been easy to CROSS over the bridge, but it has been worth it. I have been tempted to slip into depression and hopelessness many times. I have had to remind myself what God's Word says and say it out loud. I have had to remember how He expects me to respond to my circumstances, and do it. I have had to search my heart, confess my sin, and repent. I have had to choose to forgive, to love, to obey, to give thanks, and to praise Him. But as I have made those choices, I have experienced His joy and His presence, and nothing this life has to offer is better than that.

Through the struggles and tears, I have been transformed. I have been given an opportunity to become more like Christ, who learned obedience through the things He suffered (Hebrews 5:8). I have learned lessons that I wouldn't have learned any other way, and in hindsight, I'm thankful for every single one of them.

Each time we face heartache, pain, or suffering of any kind, we have an opportunity to become different, to change for the better from the inside out. We can hear and experience things during our seasons of darkness that we will never know or understand while we are in the light.

The difference between a lump of coal and a diamond is just time, heat, and pressure. When we stay in faith and persevere during times of pressure, God is able to transform us from a "lump of coal" into a stunning diamond. This transformation doesn't happen overnight. It takes time. But if we don't give up, it does happen, and a changed life is a beautiful sight to behold! It is a life full of blessings, and God receives the credit.

Through our suffering, we're also given an opportunity to receive an eternal reward. Second Corinthians 4:17 (NIV) tells us that "our light and momentary troubles are achieving for us an eternal glory that far outweighs them all." If we respond correctly, all of our troubles attain eternal rewards for us, rewards that we could not achieve any other way. The Message Bible says it like this, "these hard times are small potatoes compared to the coming good times, the lavish celebration prepared for us."

Blessings in this life are wonderful, and we can appreciate them to the fullest. But this life will be over quickly, and most of those blessings will come to an end. However, our eternal blessings will last forever! God's desire is to bless us for all eternity, not just for now. Some of our eternal rewards can only be achieved by faithfully enduring suffering.

The Bible tells us that God keeps track of all our sorrows. He records them in His book. He collects our tears! (Psalm 56:8). Why do you suppose He does that? I believe it is because He wants to repay us for each one. Jesus often talked about the rewards waiting for us. He told us that when we are persecuted, or make sacrifices for the Kingdom, or even give a cup of cold water to a little one, there will be a great reward waiting for us in Heaven. (See Matthew 5, 6, 10, 16.) Revelation 22:12 says that Jesus is coming back soon, bringing a reward to repay all people according to their deeds.

Paul told the Hebrews in Hebrews 10:34–35 (NLT), "You suffered along with those who were thrown into jail, and when all you owned was taken from you, you accepted it with joy. You knew there were better things waiting for you that will last forever. So do not throw away this confident trust in the Lord. Remember the great reward it brings you!"

Paul also spoke of our future reward in 1 Corinthians 3:14, Ephesians 6:8, Hebrews 11:26, and Galatians 6:9 (NLT), "So let's not get tired of doing what is good. At just the right time we will reap a harvest of blessing if we don't give up." First Peter 3:14 says that even if we suffer for doing what is right, God will reward us for it. The book of James encourages us to look forward to our reward as well. "God blesses those who patiently endure testing and temptation. Afterward they will receive the crown of life that God has promised to those who love him" (James 1:12, NLT).

Now imagine that all of your tears, all of your troubles and pain and the suffering that you have endured throughout this life have been collected and counted. Imagine that every moment of every day that you have chosen to remain faithful to the Lord, and you have put your trust in Him, He has prepared a reward for you to repay you for your sorrow and your suffering. You may have an incredibly large reward account already waiting for you in Heaven! I'm sure I do. The more troubles that we have to endure, the greater our eternal reward. I say, "Bring them on!" We have nothing to lose, and everything to gain!

It Is Worth It Right Now!

There is another reward that we receive, when we choose to rejoice in the middle of difficulties. We are given the privilege of seeing God in a whole new light. We may have only known Jesus as our

Savior before. But when we draw close to Him during our trials, He becomes so much greater to us. We see Him more clearly. We begin to understand that He truly is our Friend, our Shepherd, our Healer, our Deliverer, and infinitely more.

We get to know our Heavenly Father in a way that we have never known Him before as well. We understand His intense love for us as His children. We realize that He is almighty, omnipresent, and omnipotent. We get to experience a God encounter! We get to experience what Job experienced when he said in Job 42:5 (NLT), "I had heard about you before, but now I have seen you with my own eyes."

Inviting God's presence into the midst of my troubles reminds me of enjoying a cool breeze on a hot summer day. The breeze doesn't immediately change the temperature, but it makes it so much easier to bear.

When we seek God, the Holy Spirit comes like a breeze into our lives. If we give Him a restricted invitation, He will blow softly, bringing a little comfort and relief from our suffering. If we invite Him openly, He can blow more forcefully, and remove the garbage and debris from our past, giving us more freedom. But if we allow Him to have full access to our lives, He can come like a tornado, and completely destroy everything that the enemy has used against us. He has the power to change everything in an instant, and give us a brand new life if we dare to let Him.

God will not force Himself into our lives. He waits for us to invite Him and to let Him have control. The more we seek Him, the more we will learn about Him. The more we learn about Him, the more we will love Him. The more we express our love to Him, the more we will receive from Him.

God's desire is for us to know Him. He longs for us to want to be with Him. He doesn't want us to come to Him only when we want something from Him. He wants us to want *Him*. If we aren't pursuing a relationship with God, then He will pursue one with us. He loves us too much to let us go. He will do whatever it takes to get us to seek Him, and honestly, nothing forces us to seek God more than suffering.

Suffering is another way for God to reveal Himself to the world through us. Jesus said that

He is the Light of the World (John 8:12) and that if we follow Him, His light is inside us. He also said *we* are the light of the world (Matt. 5:14).

When we experience suffering, people take notice. People who otherwise might never relate to us, or have any interest in our lives, may suddenly become a friend, acquaintance, or a "follower" simply because of what we are going through. When we go through suffering with joy and peace, the glory of the Lord shines through us in a profound way. The rest of the world may be in darkness, but our love, joy and peace in the midst of it, brings a powerful light, and they are drawn to it.

> "Arise, Jerusalem! Let your light shine for all to see, for the glory of the LORD rises to shine on you. Darkness as black as night covers all the nations of the earth, but the glory of the LORD rises and appears over you. All nations will come to your light; mighty kings will come to see your radiance." (Isaiah 60:1–3, NLT)

Our adversary, the devil, will do anything he can to extinguish our light so that our light can't draw others to Christ. When our light is shining, it brings glory to God. The world can see who He is through us and they are attracted to Him. But when we let suffering steal our joy, when we express anger and resentment, or complain about our circumstances, our behavior does not reflect Christ. No one is drawn to God, and the devil wins.

Leading someone to the Lord is one of the greatest experiences you will ever have in this life! The joy a person feels when they realize that they have been used to save someone for all eternity is just indescribable. We will receive eternal rewards for everything we do for God. But when you get to have the privilege of using your testimony to help someone else, and they encounter God for the first time, that experience is its own reward. Few things in life are as satisfying and rewarding.

Live as People of Light

Chapter 5 of the apostle Paul's letter to the church in Ephesus is a fairly thorough summary of the life of a disciple of Christ. For me, this says it all. This is what our life should look like.

Ephesians 5 (NLT)

"Imitate God, therefore, in everything you do, because you are his dear children. Live a life filled with love, following the example of Christ. He loved us and offered himself as a sacrifice for us, a pleasing aroma to God.

"Let there be no sexual immorality, impurity, or greed among you. Such sins have no place among God's people. Obscene stories, foolish talk, and coarse jokes—these are not for you. Instead, let there be thankfulness to God. You can be sure that no immoral, impure, or greedy person will inherit the

Kingdom of Christ and of God. For a greedy person is an idolater, worshiping the things of this world.

"Don't be fooled by those who try to excuse these sins, for the anger of God will fall on all who disobey him. Don't participate in the things these people do. For once you were full of darkness, but now you have light from the Lord. So live as people of light! For this light within you produces only what is good and right and true. Carefully determine what pleases the Lord. Take no part in the worthless deeds of evil and darkness; instead, expose them. It is shameful even to talk about the things that ungodly people do in secret. But their evil intentions will be exposed when the light shines on them, for the light makes everything visible. This is why it is said,

"Awake, O sleeper, rise up from the dead, and Christ will give you light."

"So be careful how you live. Don't live like fools, but like those who are wise. Make the most of every opportunity in these evil days. Don't act thoughtlessly, but understand what the Lord wants you to do. Don't be drunk with wine, because that will ruin your life. Instead, be filled with the Holy Spirit, singing psalms and hymns and spiritual songs among yourselves, and making music to the Lord in your hearts. And give thanks for everything to God the Father in the name of our Lord Jesus Christ."

When we learn to practice the Greatest Commandment, by loving God and loving others (Matthew 22:37–40) we will be rewarded. Our love and obedience will enable us to endure suffering with joy and thanksgiving. People will notice our joy and God will receive the credit. Because of our lives, people will be drawn to Him. This is all God's plan, and His plan for us is the only way to experience a life that is truly worth living.

You can enjoy your life! Leave your old life behind and accept God's plan. God has a new place, a better place, for you to live. It's time to cross over and experience it!

Make it personal:

1. What does the CROSS acronym stand for?

2. What does the JOY acronym stand for?

3. If you are lacking joy, what "fruit of the spirit" do you need to practice first, before you can experience joy?

4. When should you CROSS over the bridge?

5. When you remain faithful to the Lord during your troubles, what can you expect to receive?

6. How does your joy affect others?

7. What do you need to do in order to always be joyful?

END NOTES

1. Ruth Bell Graham, *It's My Turn* (Minneapolis: Grason, 1982), 74.
2. From the Focus on the Family broadcast, "Building the Bridge to Forgiveness," Part 1 of 2, 4/02/2012.
3. Diane Moody, *Confessions of a Prayer Slacker*, 2010.

ABOUT THE AUTHOR

Deborah Ruth Cifranic has battled tremendous adversity in her life, including the heartbreak of divorce, the death of her child, financial losses, chronic pain, depression, and more. She candidly writes about her struggles and her victories, teaching biblical truths in an applicable and memorable way. Her words are personal, passionate, and practical.

Deborah is a former grade school teacher, business owner, foster parent, pastor, and worship leader. She has deep love and gratitude for her Savior, Jesus Christ, and a strong desire to help others discover a meaningful relationship with Him. She is retired and lives in Clovis, California, with her husband Mark. They have seven amazing children and five beautiful grandchildren.